DK Guide to the
OCEAN

Dr. Frances Dipper

A DK Publishing Book

LONDON, NEW YORK, MUNICH,
MELBOURNE, AND DELHI

Project Editor Simon Holland
Senior Art Editors Tory Gordon-Harris
and Claire Penny
Managing Editor Sue Leonard
Managing Art Editor Cathy Chesson
Category Publisher Mary Ling
US Editors Eileen Ramchandran
and Margaret Parrish
DTP Designer Almudena Díaz
Picture Research Jo de Gray
Jacket Design Hedi Gutt
Jacket Editor Mariza O'Keeffe
Production Angela Graef

First American edition, 2002
First paperback edition, 2006

02 03 04 05 10 9 8 7 6 5 4 3 2 1

Published in the United States by
DK Publishing, Inc.
375 Hudson Street
New York, NY 10014

Library of Congress Cataloging-in-Publication Data

Dipper, Frances, 1951–
   DK guide to the oceans / Frances Anne Dipper.-- 1st American ed.
   p. cm. -- (DK guides series)
   Summary: A guide to the ocean and the life found in it, discussing
shores, water movement, the ocean basin, climate, wildlife, and
our study of the ocean.
   ISBN-13 978-0-7894-8864-0 ISBN-10 0-7894-8864-7 (hardcover)
   ISBN-13 978-0-7566-2231-2 ISBN-10 0-7566-2231-X (pbk.)
   1. Ocean--Juvenile literature. 2. Marine sciences--Juvenile literature.
   [1. Ocean. 2. Marine life. 3. Marine sciences.] I. Title: Guide to the
   oceans. II. Title. III. Series.

GC21.5 .D555 2002
551.46--dc21
                                            2002019497

Color reproduction by GRB Editrice, S.r.l., Verona

Printed and bound in China by Toppan Printing Co., Ltd

Discover more at
www.dk.com

CONTENTS

4
ONE OCEAN

6
THE BIG BLUE

8
OCEAN MOTION

10
CREATING COASTS

12
SANDY SHORES

14
ROCKY SHORES

16
ON THE EDGE

18
CORAL REEFS

20
REEF LIFE

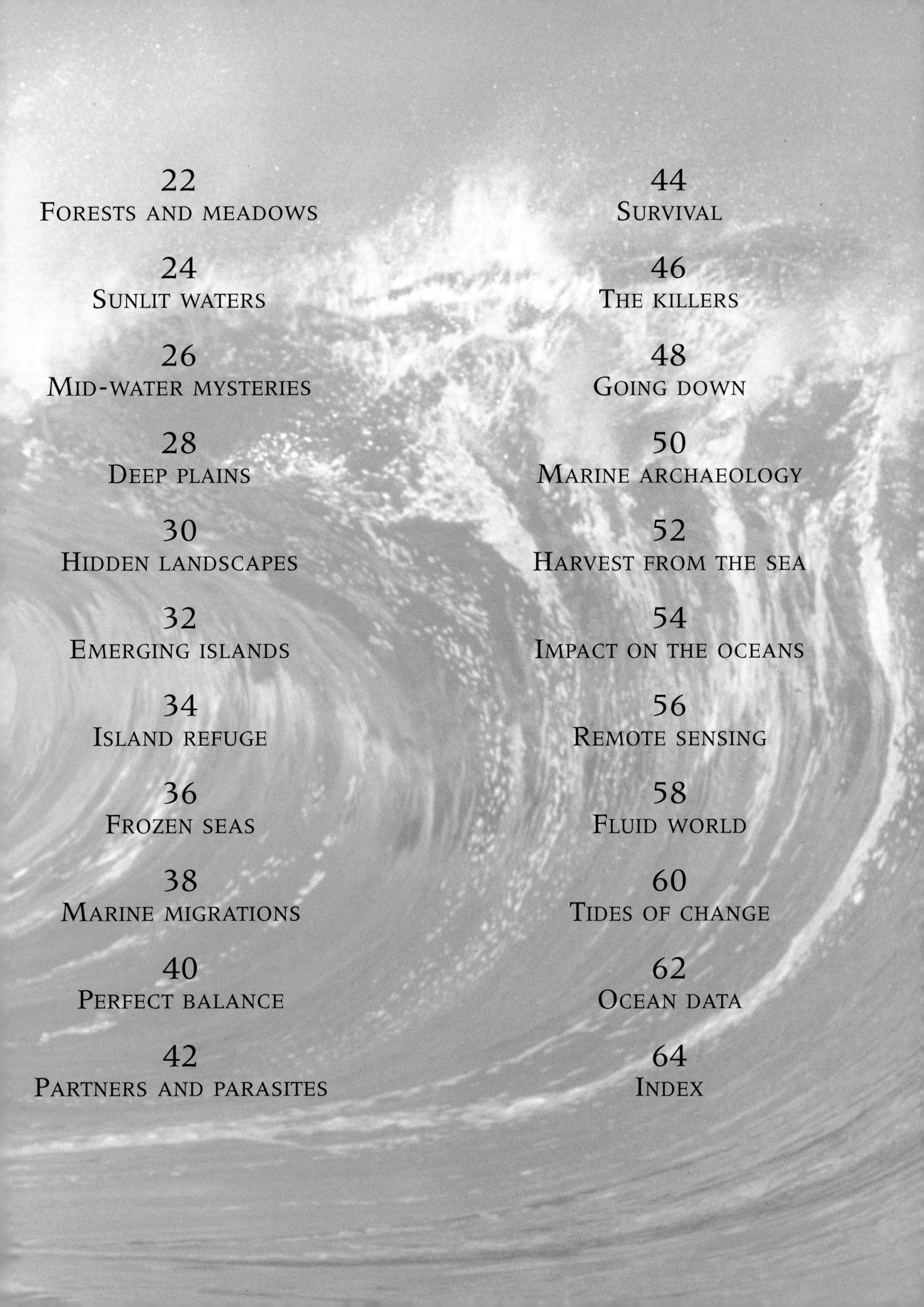

22
FORESTS AND MEADOWS

24
SUNLIT WATERS

26
MID-WATER MYSTERIES

28
DEEP PLAINS

30
HIDDEN LANDSCAPES

32
EMERGING ISLANDS

34
ISLAND REFUGE

36
FROZEN SEAS

38
MARINE MIGRATIONS

40
PERFECT BALANCE

42
PARTNERS AND PARASITES

44
SURVIVAL

46
THE KILLERS

48
GOING DOWN

50
MARINE ARCHAEOLOGY

52
HARVEST FROM THE SEA

54
IMPACT ON THE OCEANS

56
REMOTE SENSING

58
FLUID WORLD

60
TIDES OF CHANGE

62
OCEAN DATA

64
INDEX

ONE OCEAN

PHOTOGRAPHS OF THE EARTH, TAKEN FROM SPACE, clearly show the shape and position of its continents and oceans. If we had similar photographs from millions of years ago, they would show that the Earth's landmass has split and come together several times. About 250 million years ago (MYA), our continents were part of a single landmass called *Pangaea*, with a single ocean known as *Panthalassa*. When *Pangaea* split up, the ocean was also split – but the different oceans are all connected and operate as one ocean. Changes in one will eventually affect all the others.

The Tower of London, England (UK), in winter

MOVEMENT OF THE
EARTH'S CONTINENTS

200
MYA

135
MYA

10
MYA

EARTH TODAY

NORTH AMERICAN
PLATE

A line of latitude

NORTH
AMERICA

ATLANT
OCEA

PACIFIC
OCEAN

CARIBBE
PLATE

THE EQUATOR

SOUTH
AMERIC

PACIFIC PLATE

NAZCA PLATE

SO
AMER
P

The red lines indicate boundaries between tectonic plates.

SCOTIA
PLATE

ANTARCTIC PLATE

GIANT JIGSAW

Imagine that the Earth's continents are all pieces in a giant jigsaw. If you could move them around, they would all fit together quite well. The bulge on the northwestern side of Africa fits into the space between North America and South America. This is evidence that these continents were once joined together. The existence of identical fossils found on different continents also supports this theory.

The Earth's climate altered as the continents moved and as the oceans were formed. Scientists now fear that global warming may affect the oceans and currents, which would change weather patterns.

The Arabian Gulf (indicated on the map, above right) formed only 3–4 million years ago. This is very recent the geological time scale. Movements of the surroundin land caused a folding and sagging of the rocks. As a result, a shallow basin – the Gulf – was formed.

This photograph shows a shoal of chromis fish (Chromis species) above coral at the Great Barrier Reef, which extends along northeastern Australia.

CURRENT WEATHER

Ocean currents greatly influence climate and weather on land. London and Moscow should have similar climates because they are roughly the same distance away from the Equator – they have a similar "latitude" (see map). But London has much milder winters due to a current called the Gulf Stream, which carries warm water from the Caribbean to Britain. Moscow, far inland and away from the ocean, freezes up in winter with temperatures as low as 14°F (-10°C).

...ky Park in Moscow, Russia ...ssian Federation), in winter

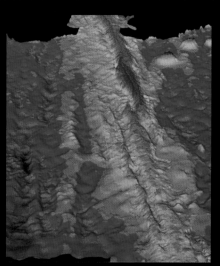

Dotted lines indicate plates and plate boundaries that scientists are not too certain about.

GROWING OCEANS

This sonar image shows the East Pacific Rise, which is part of the mid-ocean ridge that runs down the Pacific Ocean. The ridge marks the line where two tectonic plates are pulling apart and where a new area of seabed is forming between them. This part of the Pacific is slowly getting wider as a result. Dark blue indicates the deepest depths while red shows the shallowest areas.

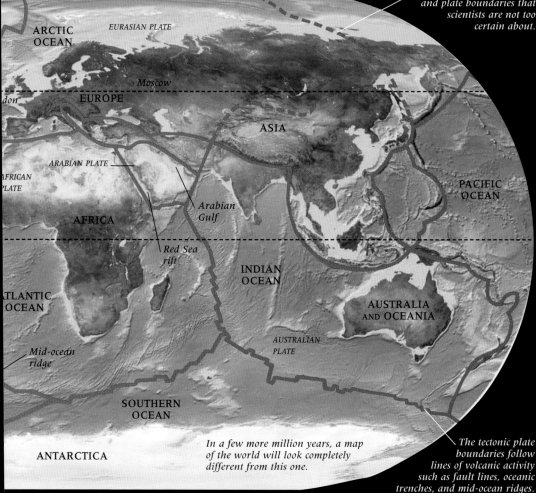

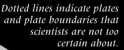

In a few more million years, a map of the world will look completely different from this one.

The tectonic plate boundaries follow lines of volcanic activity such as fault lines, oceanic trenches, and mid-ocean ridges.

...NTINENTAL DRIFT

...e Earth's continents are still moving and changing today – very, very slowly. ...s process is called continental drift. The Earth's strong outer "skin" – called ...lithosphere – is cracked, like an eggshell, into about 12 large and small ...ctonic plates." Volcanic forces deep within the Earth cause the plates to ...slide over the deeper, more liquid-like layers. In doing so, the plates ...carry the continents with them, like a giant game of "piggyback."

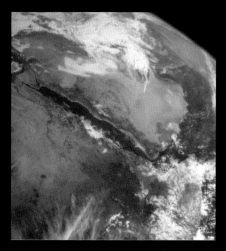

RED SEA RIFT

The Red Sea was formed about 50 million years ago, when Africa started to drift away from Arabia. This created a deep split that eventually became the Red Sea. The Red Sea is still getting wider at a rate of about 0.8 in (2 cm) per year. In 150 million years, it could even be as wide as the Atlantic Ocean.

THE BIG BLUE

THE OCEAN IS AN ENORMOUS, THREE-DIMENSIONAL living space. A lot of marine animals and plants live in or on the seabed, but many others spend their entire lives drifting or swimming near the surface and in mid-water. They have special adaptations to help them float effortlessly at their chosen depth. Most animals live within a particular depth range, but some change levels depending on whether it is day or night. In contrast, only a few specialized insects live a completely airborne life. For most of them, it takes up too much energy to stay permanently aloft in the thin air.

DIVISIONS OF THE MARINE ENVIRONMENT

Start of continental slope (650 ft)

1. SEASHORE AND SUBLITTORAL ZONE:
0–650 FT (0–200 M)

2. CONTINENTAL SLOPE:
650–13,000 FT (200–4,000 M)

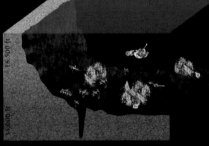

3. DEEPSEA: BED, VENTS, AND OCEAN TRENCHES

OPEN WATER ZONES

1. Sunlit or epipelagic zone, (including surface): 0–650 ft (0–200 m)

Marine life: plankton, jellyfish, flying fish, shoaling fish such as herring, fast predators such as tuna, swordfish and blue sharks, dolphins

2. Twilight or mesopelagic zone: 650–6,500 ft (200–2,000 m)

Marine life: animal plankton, small silvery fish with large eyes such as lantern fish, squid, prawns

3. Deepsea zones – bathypelagic zone and abyssopelagic zone (which includes deepsea trenches): 6,500–33,000 ft (2,000–10,000 m)

Marine life: small fish with large mouths and stomachs such as gulper eels, widemouths, anglerfish, rattail fish

THE MARINE ENVIRONMENT
Living in water is totally different from living on land. Wat is much more dense than air and provides support. The blu whale is the largest animal that has ever lived on Earth. It measure as much as 98 ft (30 m) in length. Nothing this si could ever survive on land – it would simply be too heavy move. Sound travels much faster in water than in air, whi aids communication between marine animals. Whales, for instance, can call to each other over huge distances.

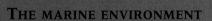

ECHINODERMS
Scientists believe that life on Earth began in the oceans and only later spread out onto the land. Most big groups (phyla) of animals found living in the sea also have representatives on land or in fresh water. Snails, for example, are found in the sea, on land, and in fresh water. However one large group, called the echinoderms (which means "spiny-skinned"), is only found in the oceans. Starfish, sea urchins, and sea cucumbers are all echinoderms.

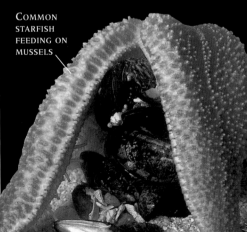

COMMON STARFISH FEEDING ON MUSSELS

SEA URCHIN

SEA CUCUM

SPERM WHALE (*PHYSETER MACROCEPHALUS*)

CRUSHING PRESSURE

Atmospheric pressure is commonly measured in units called atmospheres (atm). 1 atm is equal to about 15 lb of force per sq in (1 kg per sq cm). Going down into the depths of the oceans, water pressure increases by 1 atm for every 33 ft (10 m) of depth. Sperm whales can easily dive down to 3,300 ft (1,000 m), where the pressure – which is now 100 times greater than at the surface – crushes their chest and lungs. No human could survive this, but whales can. While underwater, they use oxygen already in their body tissues and reinflate their lungs as they surface. Animals without any air spaces inside them, such as deepsea fish, are not affected by the increased pressure.

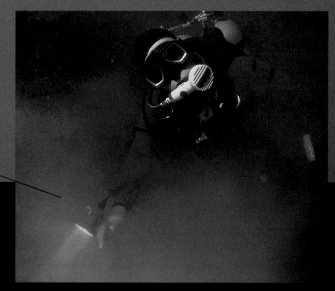

Silt stirred up by currents, waves – and divers – reduces visibility.

RED AND BLUE

Light is made up of the colors of the rainbow – red, orange, yellow, green, blue, indigo, and violet. In the ocean, red objects such as this lionfish appear a dull, bluish color (top left) – as does a diver's blood! This is because the red part of light can only penetrate a short distance down into the ocean. Artificial flash light, from an underwater camera or flashlight, restores the true color (bottom left).

FOGGY WATER

On a clear day, on land, it is possible to see mountains and hills many miles away. Even in the clearest tropical seas, a diver can only see objects up to about 164 ft (50 m) away. On land, this would be considered a thick fog! Floating plankton and silt greatly reduce visibility in coastal waters.

OCEAN MOTION

WAVES ARE GENERATED BY wind blowing across the ocean surface. Strong, long-lasting winds blowing over great distances create the biggest waves. When a wave nears land, its base catches on the seabed and slows, while the top part carries on, curls over, and crashes down as a breaker. Ocean currents, flowing like underwater winds, move water around the oceans in giant circles. Some currents are warm while others are cold, and this has a great influence on our weather.

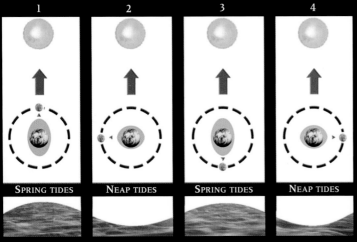

1	2	3	4
SPRING TIDES	NEAP TIDES	SPRING TIDES	NEAP TIDES

DIRECTED BY THE MOON

Tides are caused by the pull of gravity from the Sun and the Moon. The Moon is nearer to the Earth and so it exerts a stronger pull. The Moon moves around the Earth, and when the Sun, Moon, and Earth are in line, 1 and 3, their gravities act together. This causes very high and low tides – the "spring" tides. When the Sun and Moon lie at right angles, 2 and 4, the pull is weaker and there are smaller tides – the "neap" tides.

High tide in the Bay of Fundy   *Low tide in the Bay of Fundy*

HIGH AND DRY

Tides do not all behave the same around all the oceans' shores. In some places, such as the Mediterranean, the difference between the highest and the lowest water levels (the tidal range) is only about 3.3 ft (1 m) and the tide does not go out very far. In contrast, the tide in the Bay of Fundy, in Canada, falls by around 46 ft (14 m) and a huge expanse of seabed is revealed twice a day – leaving the boats there high and dry (above).

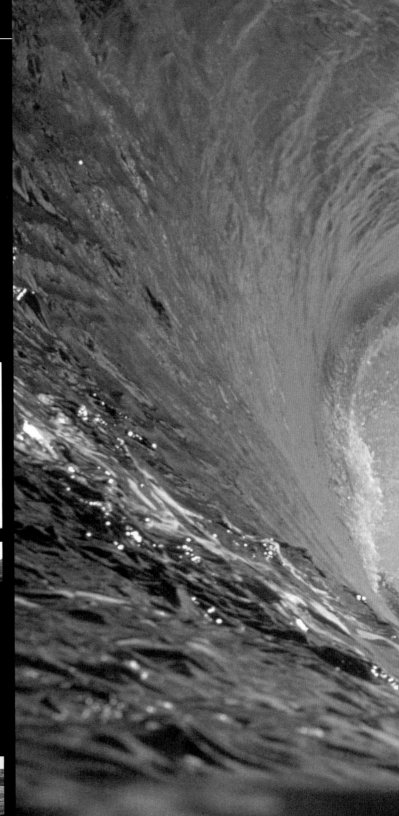

OCEAN SURFING

While most people fear the tremendous power of the huge breakers that roll onto the shores of Hawaii, surfers use this energy to experience the ride of a lifetime. With perfect timing and balance, a few expert surfers have skied down the smooth front of *Jaws*, the most dangerous and challenging wave system in the world – and lived to tell the tale. *Jaws* rears up to 60 ft (18 m) high along the edge of a hidden offshore reef near Maui, Hawaii. Most ocean waves are less than 12 ft (3.7 m) high.

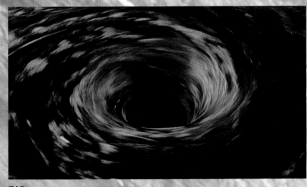

WHIRLPOOLS

Whirlpools like this one (above) are created when strong tidal currents meet and clash. This usually happens where the water is channeled through narrow passages between islands and landmasses. Water roars so fast through the Saltstraumen Channel, off Norway's northwestern coast, that the noise of the resulting whirlpools and eddies – where the water current reverses back on itself – can be heard several miles away.

Surfing waves this big is exhilarating but dangerous. The huge downward force and weight of the breaking wave can crush both people and boats.

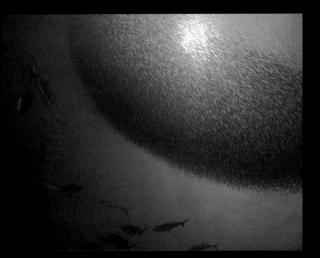

CURRENT FOOD

Water currents can move up and down as well as sideways. Upwelling currents carry vital nutrients from the depths up to the surface. The nutrients provide food for tiny floating plants and animals (plankton), which multiply rapidly and are, in turn, eaten by small fish. Plankton in strong, upwelling currents off the coast of Peru feed gigantic shoals of silvery anchovies. Millions of these tiny fish are themselves caught by larger fish, birds, and fishermen. Nearly a quarter of all the fish caught worldwide are taken from here.

This picture was taken during a tsunami that hit Hilo Bay, Hawaii, in 1960.

TSUNAMIS

For over 27,000 Japanese people living along the coast, June 26, 1896, was the last day of their lives. A huge wave, more than 100 ft (30.5 m) high, engulfed their villages and homes. Like most tsunamis, or tidal waves, this one was triggered by an undersea earthquake. The violent shaking of the seabed creates fast-moving waves that radiate outward. Racing toward the coast, waves pile into one another when they reach shallow water and a huge, destructive tsunami is formed. The term *tsunami* (pronounced "su-naa-mee") is a Japanese word meaning "harbor wave."

CREATING COASTS

AROUND THE WORLD'S COASTS, an endless battle is fought where land meets sea. Every wave that crashes against the beach slowly wears it away. The damage is done by the sand, rocks, and debris that the waves fling against the shore. Soft sandstone and chalk cliffs are eroded quickly, while hard granite cliffs will hardly change over hundreds of years. On sheltered coasts, where waves are small, the sea may add land instead of taking it away. Currents and waves carry sediment in from deeper water and drop it in quiet, inshore areas. Sand and shingle bars, mud flats, and river deltas are built this way.

THE APOSTLES

Port Campbell National Park in the state of Victoria, Australia, is famous for its scenery. Twelve rocky stacks known as the *Apostles*, stand like sentries guarding the rugged coastline. Each rock was once part of a headland that had been sculpted into an arch by the sea. Continual battering by waves broke each arch, leaving these dramatic rocks standing free.

This stack will eventually collapse into smaller pieces as its base is worn away by crashing waves. Meanwhile, new stacks are being created at other headlands.

UNDESIRABLE RESIDENCE

This house on the Norfolk coast in England was once a long way from the cliff edge. Waves have eroded the soft coastline, over many years, so that some ancient village sites are now several miles out to sea. Rock breakwaters have been built offshore at Sea Palling to help stop further erosion.

STEMMING THE TIDE

Building sea walls, such as this one in the US, protects seaside towns from the full force of the pounding waves. But this can also cause erosion problems farther down the coast if the wave patterns and water flow are altered.

ANIMAL EROSION

Cliffs and shores made of soft rock are eroded by shellfish such as piddocks. The animals drill into the rock when they are small and enlarge their holes as they grow.

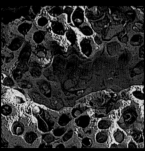

The Fleet is a brackish (slightly salty) lagoon cut off by Chesil Beach. Its quiet, shallow waters hide some fascinating and rare marine creatures.

BUILDING STONES

Walking the length of Chesil Beach in Dorset, England, is extremely tiring! This bank of shingle was built entirely by the sea and stretches for 18 miles (29 km) between the Isle of Portland and the mainland. Strong waves move the pebbles along the coast and toss them up onto the shore.

CAVES AND GULLEYS

Coastlines that are exposed to the full force of ocean waves are often full of caves, carved out by the impact of the waves and the debris they carry. This spectacular blowhole in Hawaii was formed by waves pushing air and water into a small cave in a rock platform. The explosive force created inside the cave literally blew the roof off, creating an escape hole. With the exit hole clear, the air and water mixture can now be blown high into the air.

A diver shines his flashlight as he peers down into the blue water.

BLUE HOLES

Divers on the island of Gozo, Malta – in the Mediterranean – can walk into a beautiful pool in the shore, dive down into it, and swim out underwater through a huge archway. Over the centuries, this "blue hole" was carved out of fossilized rock by stormy seawaters. Some blue holes in the Bahamas open a long way inland.

SANDY SHORES

A SANDY BEACH IS A PERFECT PLACE to have a picnic, play games, and build sandcastles. This habitat is also a wonderful environment for wildlife. Compared to a rocky shore, the sand may appear lifeless. Seaweeds, limpets, and other fixed animals cannot attach themselves to the shifting surface. Instead, the animals live beneath the surface, protected from storms and safe from birds and other predators. The strand line left behind, as the tide goes out, provides clues as to what lives both here and farther out to sea. Shells, egg cases, bones, seaweeds, fishing nets, and other debris are picked over by birds, crabs, and even foxes.

Common seals (Phoca vitulina) are also known as harbor seals.

NATURAL SWIMMERS

Common seal pups are often born on sandbars and sandy beaches that appear at low tide. They are able to swim within a few minutes of being born and thus are not in danger of drowning when the tide comes in. The pups shed their first white coat before they are born, so they are not often hunted for their skins.

HUMAN TIDE

Sandy shores near towns and cities attract thousands of vacationers, especially in warmer climates. This crowded beach in Hawaii is typical. When large numbers of people trample over sand dunes, they can loosen or kill the vegetation that holds the dunes together. As a result, whole dunes may disappear when the wind blows.

HIDDEN VARIETY

Gazing along a sandy shore at low tide, it is hard to imagine that anything can live in such a bare desert. In fact, a surprising variety of worms, shells, crabs, starfish, and urchins lie safely hidden in the damp sand. When the tide returns, these animals emerge to feed.

peacock worm
ella pavonina)
ds a beautiful fan
tacles from its muddy
At the slightest sign of
r, it instantly retreats
down its tube.

Ragworms are a favorite food of many wading birds – so, when the tide is out, they burrow into the sand to avoid being eaten. However, they themselves are also active hunters that search out their prey. Fishermen dig them out for bait – but, if handled carelessly, their powerful black jaws can give a painful nip.

SAND CREATURES

Sand is made of such small particles it is difficult to separate the individual grains. But, believe it or not, a whole community of animals – known as the meiofauna – lives in the water-filled spaces between the sand grains. The most common type are tiny worms such as the one shown here (*Derocheilocaris typica*, above) and minute, shrimp-like animals called copepods.

NATTERJACK TOAD

Although relatively common in western Europe, the natterjack toad (*Bufo calamita*) is rare in Britain, where it survives only in sand dunes and heaths. Here, it can burrow easily and lay its eggs in warm, freshwater pools at the back of the dunes.

Marram grass is holding these sand dunes together with its long roots and runners. Shifting sand stimulates it to grow upward and send out side shoots.

Below is a sand mountain built by a male ghost crab (Ocypode quadrata) at the top of a beach in Oman. The crab lives in the burrow next door (bottom right). The tower (below left) is the marker for his territory.

ND GHOSTS

k along a sandy, tropical shore as dusk falls
you will not be alone! Ghost crabs scurry
l directions, running swiftly on their long
. They blend into the background so well
, if they stop, they seem to
opear. This is how they got
r name. These crabs feed
debris brought in by
n tide.

ROCKY SHORES

As the tide goes down on a rocky shore, it uncovers a hidden seascape of rocks, cliffs, gulleys, and pools. Rocky shores in temperate (cool) regions, such as Great Britain and North America, are home to hundreds of different creatures. Masses of slippery brown seaweeds lie strewn in tangled heaps as the water drains away. Snails and crabs creep into damp crevices. Barnacles, mussels, and limpets stop feeding and tightly close up their shells to keep the life-giving seawater inside.

Green and brown seaweeds in an intertidal area along a temperate, rocky seashore on Bardsey Island, North Wales (UK). The brown seaweeds produce a slimy substance called mucilage, which protects them from the wind and sunshine at low tide.

TIDAL TERRAIN
Exactly what sorts of plants and animals live on a rocky shore depends on where in the world the shore is. Seaweeds grow well on this shore on Bardsey Island, in North Wales (UK). In the picture, low spring tides have uncovered a part of the shore normally hidden from view, so that a kelp forest is revealed. A similar shore in the tropics would have very few plants. Exposed to the hot sunshine while the tide was out, such plants would soon die.

The sea scorpion (Myoxocephalus scorpius), below, can change its color to suit the background.

SHORE TO BE A SAFE PLACE
Sheltered rocky shores are home to a wide variety of small fish, which hide among seaweeds and in pools. However, it is surprisingly difficult to spot them. As long as they do not move, they are safe from predators such as this sharp-eyed heron.

BLACK-CROWNED NIGHT HERON

LITTLE SUCKERS

On rough, wave-exposed shores, seaweeds cannot grow well and so, instead, the rocks are covered with barnacles, limpets, and mussels. Limpets can cling on so tightly that it is almost impossible to dislodge them. Protected by their tough shells, periwinkles are rolled by the waves into crevices, while starfish grip on to rocks using thousands of tube feet, which act as suckers.

With the tide in, this limpet (Patella species) can glide around, grazing on algae and leaving beautiful patterns of "teeth marks" on the rocks (above).

PERIWINKLES

ROCK POOLS

Rock pools are like miniature oases on the seashore, where delicate fish, anemones, and other soft animals can survive at low tide. However, living in a rock pool can be quite difficult. Small pools heat up and get very salty as the water evaporates on hot summer days. They also get diluted by rainwaters, which makes the water too fresh for many marine animals, and in winter small pools can freeze over. Pools high up on the shore pose the most difficult living conditions.

STARFISH IN ROCK POOL (USA)

These ocher sea stars (Pisaster ochraceus) are common in rock pools and on seashores in the US. They vary in color from orange to a greenish hue.

DUTIFUL DAD

The lumpsucker (*Cyclopterus lumpus*) visits northern European shores in late winter. The female lays her eggs, sticking them carefully onto a rock. But it is the male that stays behind to guard them. A strong sucker on his belly helps him to stay near the eggs when powerful waves come surging up the shore.

The pink and orange colors of the male lumpsucker are especially bright during the breeding season.

ON THE EDGE

Whardware **W**HEN THE TIDE GOES OUT along a mangrove-
fringed shore, it reveals an almost alien
landscape. Instead of a forest floor carpeted with
leaves, humans and animals are faced by an almost
impenetrable tangle of prop
roots, which hang down, and
aerial roots that grow up into
the air instead of down into the
soil! The prop roots support the
trees while the aerial roots keep salt
out and help the tree to breathe in salt
water, which is normally fatal to land
plants. Mangrove forests fringe muddy
shores in tropical areas of the world.

MANGROVE
SNAKE

*These mud flats in Liverpool Bay, England (UK), provide
wading birds with a feast of worms and shellfish.*

BIRD LARDERS

Many northern European countries have coastlines with lots
of river estuaries. Here, where fresh water meets salt water, great
expanses of mud are deposited as the river drops its sediment
load. At low tide, these mud flats provide feeding grounds for
huge flocks of birds. British estuaries are important since they lie
on the migration route for ducks, geese, and wading birds that
fly south to spend the winter in the Mediterranean and Africa.

CRAB-EATING
MACAQUE

HUNTING GROUND

Mangrove forests are a
natural pantry full of birds,
insects, fish, crabs, and
snails – an excellent hunting
ground for those animals
that can find a way in.
Where mangroves merge
into tropical rain forest,
monkeys such as the
crab-eating macaque
are common. Fruit
bats roost in the
dense branches and
estuarine crocodiles
penetrate deep into
the forest through twisting
mangrove channels.

CARDINAL
FISH

OYSTERS

PROP
ROOTS

SEA LAVENDER

ESSEX SKIPPER
BUTTERFLY

SEA DEFENSES

In cool areas such as northern Europe, there are no mangroves. Instead, sheltered, muddy shores are often bordered by salt marshes. Salt-tolerant plants such as sea lavender grow over the marshes, which are rich in wildlife. Salt marshes and mangroves both form vital sea defenses, helping to stop erosion and flooding. They can adjust to rising sea levels by growing farther inland.

RIVER DELTAS

This aerial view of the Volga River delta shows how land is formed where a mighty river meets the sea. The river carries mud particles that settle on the seabed and build up into banks. As these become higher, plants colonize the mud and stabilize it, forming a delta crossed by many river channels. Human settlements on dry deltas are at serious risk from flooding.

TREE FISH

Finding a fish on land is surprising enough, but finding one in a tree is truly extraordinary! Mudskippers climb up mangrove tree branches as the tide comes in, to avoid predatory fish. They use their strong front fins like arms and cling on with a sucker situated on their belly.

While out of water, mudskippers keep their gills full of a frothy mixture of air and water so that they can still breathe. At low tide, they drop off the trees to feed on creatures in the mud flats.

DERWATER NURSERY

tangle of underwater roots and branches
g the seaward edge of this mangrove forest,
e US, provides a safe home for small fish.
y juvenile fish, including young sharks and
racuda, use the mangroves as a nursery area.
y when they are large enough to defend
nselves will they venture out into
open ocean.

17

CORAL REEFS

THE GREAT BARRIER REEF IS ONE OF the longest reefs in the world. It extends for more than 1,240 miles (2,000 km) along the northeastern coast of Australia. It seems incredible that this huge structure – visible from space – was built by tiny coral animals (polyps) less than 0.4 in (1 cm) high. Thousands of these polyps live, joined together, inside every coral.

CORAL ATOLL FORMATION

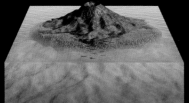

Coral atolls start life as fringing reefs growing around volcanic islands far out in the ocean.

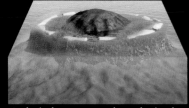

Geological processes and weathering have caused the volcano to sink and disappear, leaving a ring of coral behind it.

Sand and rubble build islands on top of the coral. Larger islands are colonized by plants and animals.

CORAL REEF FORMATIONS

Coral reefs can only grow in shallow waters, where there is a hard seabed to which they can attach themselves. This is why most reefs grow along the edges of continents (barrier reefs) or around islands (fringing reefs). This fringing reef (below) is typical of those surrounding islands throughout Micronesia, in the Pacific Ocean.

NATURAL PREDATORS

The prickly crown-of-thorns starfish eats living coral. Whole reefs can be killed when large numbers invade an area. Sitting on top of the coral, the starfish extends its stomach out through its mouth and digests the soft coral polyps.

Lophelia pertusa

Brightly colored soft corals and sponges grow among the white Lophelia coral.

COLD WATER CORALS

Deep down in the cold, dark waters off Norway and western Scotland there are also coral reefs! These reefs consist of only one type of hard coral – *Lophelia*. This coral grows slowly as it does not contain *zooxanthellae* (tiny plants), which provide extra food for growth.

BOMBS AWAY

In Malaysia, Indonesia, and the Philippines, irresponsible fishermen toss homemade bombs onto reefs to stun and kill fish. Unfortunately, the bomb blast also smashes up the coral, which may take many years to regrow. Sometimes the fishermen themselves are injured. With the reef gone, fishing will be poor for other fishermen.

CORAL LANDSCAPES

This photograph shows the beautiful coral landscape that surrounds Komodo Island in Indonesia. The corals grow well in the clear, sunlit waters of this region. Although they are animals, coral polyps need light to build their massive skeletons. This is because the polyps carry single-celled algae called *zooxanthellae* inside their bodies. These minute plants use the energy in sunlight to make their own food and pass some of it on to the coral polyps.

REEF LIFE

A VISIT TO A CORAL REEF is an amazing experience for divers to enjoy. A healthy reef simply bursts with life and color in just the same way that a tropical rain forest does on land. Even a small reef in the Indian Ocean may have many hundreds of different sorts of corals, fish, crabs, starfish, sea urchins, and other animals. Millions of people in coastal communities worldwide rely on coral reefs to provide fish, medicines, and many other materials. But reefs are important to all of us. Corals use up carbon dioxide to make their skeletons and thus help to prevent global warming.

These whitetip reef sharks are hunting surgeonfish in coral around Cocos Island, Costa Rica.

PURPLE TUBE
SPONGE

A beautiful purple tube sponge from the Caribbean. Sponges come in a wide variety of shapes and colors and are common on most coral reefs.

EMPEROR
ANGELFISH

RED SEA REEFS

The coral reef scene shown in the main photograph (above) is typical of the Red Sea. The corals come in many different shapes and sizes and jostle with one another for space. Each coral colony has grown up from a single small larva that drifted in and settled on the reef. Clouds of small, pink anthias fish are "picking" plankton from the water, while emperor angelfish search for sponges to eat.

SHARK PATROL

This photograph, from Cocos Island in the Pacific Ocean, shows a pack of whitetip reef sharks (*Trianodon obesus*) hunting at night. During the day, the sharks rest peacefully in sandy coral caves and gullies – but as darkness falls, they burst into frenetic activity, sniffing out coral fish hidden deep in the reef.

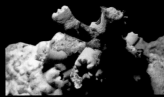
Tubastrea *coral with polyps retracted*

Tubastrea *coral with polyps extended*

FISHING AT NIGHT

Divers visiting a coral reef at night are often amazed at how colorful the corals appear in their flashlight beams. This is because it is at night that the coral polyps extend their bright tentacles to feed. During these hours of darkness, tiny plankton animals, on which the corals feed, swim up onto the reef from deeper water.

BLACKTIP
REEF SHARK

The blacktip reef shark (Carcharhinus melanopterus) hunts over shallow reefs for fish, squid, and octopuses, sometimes within an arm's length of the shore.

CORAL RELATIVES

Colorful soft corals, such as these *Dendronepthya* species from Fiji, are close relatives of reef-forming corals. As their name suggests, they do not have a hard skeleton and collapse into a soggy heap when out of water. Unlike true corals, they do not need sunlight and can live on the deeper, darker parts of the reef.

TUBE WORMS

TUBE
WORM

Coral polyps are not the only animals to make reefs. The beautiful red worm (*Serpula vermicularis*) shown on the left lives in European coastal waters. In some sheltered Scottish sea lochs, these worms grow so well that they form mini-reefs with their hard, chalky tubes.

FORESTS AND MEADOWS

WITHIN EASY REACH of the teeming bustle of many European and American cities, there are immense, tranquil forests. These forests lie not on land but under the sea and are formed by giant seaweeds known as kelp. Giant Californian kelp can reach nearly 197 ft (60 m) long. These huge plants provide a habitat for a wide variety of fish, which in turn are hunted by seals, sea lions, and dolphins. Kelp forests grow only in cool, sunlit waters and are not found in the tropics. European kelps shed their tops each year just as trees lose their leaves.

Harbor seals (right) rest and play in the kelp forest, safe from the predatory sharks that patrol the open waters farther out to sea.

SEA MEADOWS

Cows grazing peacefully in a grassy meadow are a common sight on land – but, surprisingly, you might come across a similar scene underwater! Sea grasses, which look quite like ordinary grass, grow on shallow, sandy seabeds – often covering large areas next to mangroves and coral reefs. In northern Australia and Southeast Asia, sea grass meadows are the favorite haunts of sea cows. European sea grass beds are extensively grazed by brent geese.

SAFE HAVEN

Baby lemon sharks are born live, but their mother does not look after them. In the open ocean, they would be very vulnerable to predators, so the sharks give birth to them in safe areas such as sea grass beds in shallow lagoons.

A dugong or sea cow (Dugong dugon), left, munching happily on an undersea lawn of sea grass.

SEAHORSES

Sunlight filters through the dense canopy of a giant kelp (Macrocystis) forest off the coast of California. Air bladders (small capsules of gas along the kelp) help to keep the plants upright in the water.

A close search through clumps of sea grass may reveal some of the many small creatures that live there. Seahorses thrive on tiny shrimps that dart through

SEA OTTERS

Californian giant kelp forests are home to the delightful sea otter. These charming creatures are vital predators of kelp pests. Diving down to the seabed, this otter (below) has collected a sea urchin, cracked it open with a rock, and is now busy munching into its tasty insides. Without the otters, sea urchins can overgraze and destroy large areas of kelp forest.

Giant kelp can grow up to 2 ft (0.6 m) in length every day. This growth rate is almost as quick as giant bamboo, the fastest-growing plant on land.

GIANT
KELP

HUMAN
BEING

PLANT-LIKE ANIMALS

Anemones, sponges, and sea squirts are all examples of marine animals that look and behave rather like plants. Instead of searching for their food, they can stay fixed in one spot because water currents carry tiny, floating planktonic creatures into their reach. The understory in a kelp forest has many such animals.

Soft corals such as these European dead man's fingers grow as fixed colonies. Hundreds of individual feeding heads, called polyps (left), catch passing plankton.

Colorful anemones often form part of the undergrowth in kelp forests. Their stinging tentacles can capture small fish and shrimps.

ANIMAL HOMES

Kelp plants provide a home for many small animals that live and feed on them. Hundreds of different species have been counted living on a single plant! In the photograph (above), a group of beautiful blue-rayed limpets are chewing holes in a kelp stem, which may eventually snap.

SUNLIT WATERS

THE SUNLIT SURFACE WATERS of the oceans teem with life. Huge numbers of microscopically small plants and animals, the plankton, drift in the water currents. Almost all life in the oceans ultimately depends on this floating food source. Shoals of silvery fish feed on the plankton, closely followed by hungry sharks, sailfish, and other predators. Larger jellyfish and other floating animals are blown along the surface by ocean winds.

DIVING BIRDS
Guillemots spend much of their life out at sea, feeding, resting, and sleeping on the ocean surface. They only come ashore to breed – in noisy colonies on steep cliffs. The birds fish for sprats, sand eels, and herring by dipping under the surface and then swimming underwater by flapping their wings. They can easily swim to a depth of 66 ft (20 m), and some reach nearly 650 ft (200 m)!

TOOTHLESS WONDER
The whale shark is the largest fish in the sea and can grow to at least 46 ft (14 m) long – the size of a bus! If it had teeth, like other sharks, it could eat a person in one bite. Luckily, its huge mouth is simply used to take in gallons of seawater containing the tiny shrimps, and other plankton, on which it feeds.

SARGASSUM FROGFISH IN SARGASSUM WEED

FLOATING FORESTS

The surface of the Sargasso Sea, near Bermuda, is still and warm for most of the year. These conditions have allowed a strange, floating forest to develop – a vast, tangled raft of seaweed held up by gas-filled bladders. Sea snails, urchins, and limpets graze on the seaweed, while sea snakes hunt for fish and shrimps.

A shoal of jackfish (Caranx sexfasciatus), otherwise known as big-eye trevally

SAFETY SHOALS

Fish living in sunlit surface waters protect themselves from predatory fish and seabirds by forming large shoals. When attacked, all the fish in the shoal move together and confuse the predator. Their darker backs and silvery bellies help to camouflage them from both above and below.

OCEAN WANDERERS

Leatherback turtles are true ocean wanderers. Satellite tags fitted to these gentle giants have shown that they travel thousands of miles in search of food. They can grow to nearly 6.5 ft (2 m) long and weigh up to 1,430 lb (650 kg), all on a diet consisting mainly of jellyfish.

The violet sea snail builds itself a floating "raft" by entangling air bubbles in slimy mucus.

DRIFTING FREE

While most sea snails live on the seabed, the violet sea snail (*Janthina janthina*) is completely at home drifting at the ocean surface. It feeds on other ocean drifters such as the blue jelly *Porpita* and the by-the-wind-sailor *Velella*.

MID-WATER MYSTERIES

IMAGINE FLOATING WEIGHTLESS IN DARK, COLD WATER with nothing to tell you which way is up or down. Many animals spend their entire lives swimming or drifting in mid-water, where there is very little or no light. So how do the animals find food or a mate? Some fish and crustaceans have enormous eyes to use what little light there is. Others have tiny eyes but an excellent sense of smell and antennae sensitive to vibrations.

BIOLUMINESCENCE
Bioluminescence is a beautiful, bluish light produced by living animals and plants. In the deep mid-waters, many fish, squid, jellies, and crustaceans light up with this eerie glow, which they use to navigate, hunt, signal, frighten, and even to camouflage themselves. The light is created when a chemical called luciferin is mixed with oxygen.

The anglerfish uses this glowing lure, like a fishing rod, to entice prey. It appears ferocious but, like most deepsea fish, it is only inches long.

FLASHLIGHT FISH

This fish keeps bioluminescent bacteria in special sacs under each eye. The bacteria glow constantly, but the fish can blink the lights on and off using a flap of skin.

INKY LIGHT
Many different species of squid live in the mid-water darkness and are eaten by predatory fish – if the fish can catch them. Most are only inches long, but they shimmer and glow with hundreds of tiny, bioluminescent lights. Some can even squirt out a luminous, inky "smokescreen."

This small squid, called Histioteuthis, waits quietly for passing prey to bump into its tentacles.

CREEPY HITCHHIKER
There are no solid surfaces to cling onto and make a home of in mid-water. The *Phronima* – a small, shrimp-like animal – steals itself a floating home. Gripping on to a floating sea squirt (salp) or jelly, this ingenious creature eats the insides of its prey and then uses the transparent skin as a shelter for itself and its young.

WHY RED?
This red shrimp (*Pasiphaea* species) lives in deep, dark waters lit only by bioluminescent glows. Red light does not penetrate this deep, and so red things appear black. In mid-water, therefore, the shrimp is almost invisible. However, a small, black fish called *Malosteus* captures and eats these shrimps by locating them with a beam of *red* bioluminescence.

Slipping in and out of its floating "barrel," the Phronima *can search for food in safety.*

LIVING GIANTS

In 1976, American scientists on a research ship were amazed when a 15 ft (4.5 m) long shark was hauled up from the depths entangled in their sea anchor. It was a completely new species that was soon nicknamed the "megamouth." This shark has a huge, luminous mouth that may help attract the tiny shrimps and plankton on which it feeds. Large fish such as this are very rare in the ocean's mid-waters, where food is scarce.

DEEP PLAINS

ONLY 150 YEARS AGO, biologists still believed that no marine creatures could possibly survive below a depth of 3,300 ft (1,000 m) because of the huge pressures and icy cold. The deepsea vehicles *Trieste* and *Kaiko* have since visited the very deepest part of the ocean and seen animals there. Much of the deep ocean floor consists of immense plains of soft mud, peppered with holes and mounds made by buried worms and other small animals. There are far fewer large predatory animals, such as starfish, because food is very scarce.

ELBOWS ON THE TABLE

Tripodfish "perch" just above the mud surface by propping themselves up on the tips of their long tail and front fins. Sensitive antennae help them to detect and pounce on passing small fish and shrimps.

TRIPODFISH

UNDERWATER VACUUM CLEANERS

Believe it or not, this strange-looking creature – a sea cucumber – is a close relative of the familiar starfish. Sea cucumbers are common on the muddy, deepsea floor all over the world. They get by very well here because they "vacuum" the surface, sucking in a mixture of mud and edible snacks. Undigested mud passes through their gut and is left in neat little piles, called fecal casts.

DEEPSEA SEA CUCUMBER

The sea pens shown in this picture are examples of a deepsea variety known as the "droopy" sea pen.

BLUNTNOSE SIX-GILL SHARK
(*HEXANCHUS GRISEUS*)

MIDNIGHT SNACK

On the great African plains there are plenty of antelope for swift land predators, such as cheetahs, to hunt and kill. In contrast, there are very few large hunters down on the deepsea plains. Chasing prey uses up a lot of energy and food is scarce. The bluntnose six-gill shark (above) scavenges for leftovers in the depths during the day, but hunts its live prey at night near the surface, where more food is available.

DEEPSEA BONANZA

One of the reasons there is not much food available on deep plains is that most of it gets eaten by mid-water animals on the way down. But on rare occasions, something really large, such as a dead whale, may reach the deepsea floor. Scavenging rattail fish, hagfish, and deepsea sharks – the "vultures" of the ocean depths – smell the carrion and move in for a feast.

Rattail fish get their name from their long, thin tails. They feed on anything they can catch – whether it is alive or dead.

DEEPLY DELICATE

Delicate deepsea animals such as this pom-pom anemone (*Liponema brevicornis*) are known mainly from photographs taken from submersibles. Collecting specimens using clumsy submersible arms is very difficult. In addition, many specimens disintegrate on the way to the surface because of the changing temperature and pressure.

POM-POM
ANEMONE

OISED PENS

ea cucumbers and crabs crawl and plow their way rough the muddy floor of the ocean's abyssal ains in search of things to eat. Meanwhile, ant-like animals, such as the floppy sea pens in is photograph, filter the water currents to catch ifting food. These sea pens have long, flexible alks to keep them well above the soft mud that ight otherwise clog up their mouths and tentacles.

HIDDEN LANDSCAPES

ONE OF THE BEST WAYS OF SEEING the Earth's wonderful landscape of mountains, deserts, cities, and forests is to fly over it on a clear, sunny day. Over the oceans, only the water's surface would be visible. But take the water away and you would be flying over mountains higher than Everest, steep trenches many times deeper than the Grand Canyon, and endless, flat, muddy plains more spacious than the Sahara desert.

THE OCEAN FLOOR

Following the invention of sonar and echo sounding equipment in the 1920s, it became possible to map the main features of the ocean floor, such as those shown in this diagram (below). Such devices measure the depth of the seabed, and what type it is, using sound. However, only a few areas have so far been mapped in detail, and it is still quite possible to discover unknown underwater mountains and extinct volcanoes.

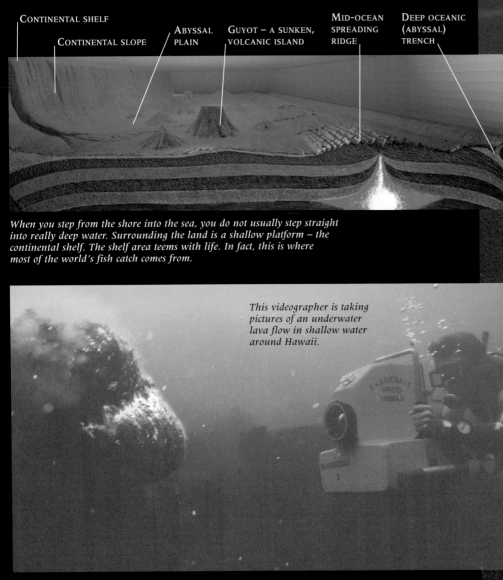

CONTINENTAL SHELF

CONTINENTAL SLOPE

ABYSSAL PLAIN

GUYOT – A SUNKEN, VOLCANIC ISLAND

MID-OCEAN SPREADING RIDGE

DEEP OCEANIC (ABYSSAL) TRENCH

When you step from the shore into the sea, you do not usually step straight into really deep water. Surrounding the land is a shallow platform – the continental shelf. The shelf area teems with life. In fact, this is where most of the world's fish catch comes from.

This videographer is taking pictures of an underwater lava flow in shallow water around Hawaii.

MID-OCEAN RIDGES

Chains of underwater mountains run the length of all the major oceans. These mid-ocean ridges may be several thousand miles wide, with peaks of up to 2.5 miles (4 km) high. Along each ridge, lava bubbles up and a new sea floor is formed as the seabed moves away on either side

A MOUNTS

...tted around the world's oceans are thousands of sea ...unts. Sea mounts are submerged, extinct volcanoes ...t may rise several miles above the ocean floor. Those ...t were once near the sea surface have flat tops and ...called guyots. Most oceanic islands are the tops of ...volcanoes. They have steep sides that drop quickly ...wn into very deep water. This photograph shows ...eep drop-off in Fiji, in the Pacific Ocean.

Kaiko, a Remotely Operated Vehicle (ROV)

TRENCH WARFARE

The deepest parts of the ocean are the abyssal trenches. The deepest of these is the Mariana Trench near the Philippines. On January 23, 1960, Donald Walsh and Jacques Piccard sank to 35,800 ft (10,900 m) – the bottom of the world – in their bathyscape, named the *Trieste*. Since then, only an unmanned Japanese ROV, called *Kaiko*, has returned there.

UNDERWATER OASES

The discovery of hydrothermal vents in the 1970s amazed marine scientists. These vents pour out super-heated water filled with minerals – known as "black smoke" – and are powered by volcanic activity. Bacteria thrive on the minerals and provide food for the many strange animals that live around the vents. Other vent animals prey on each other. Thus, the whole community survives without getting any energy from plants and sunlight.

This photograph (right) of the Saracen's Head "black smoker" vent was taken by scientists on board the submersible Alvin, *at a depth of 10,200 ft (3,100 m) on the mid-Atlantic Ridge.*

Giant deepsea clams (Calyptogena magnifica) and squat lobsters live around vents at a depth of 8,500 ft (2,600 m) off Mazatlán, Mexico.

EMERGING ISLANDS

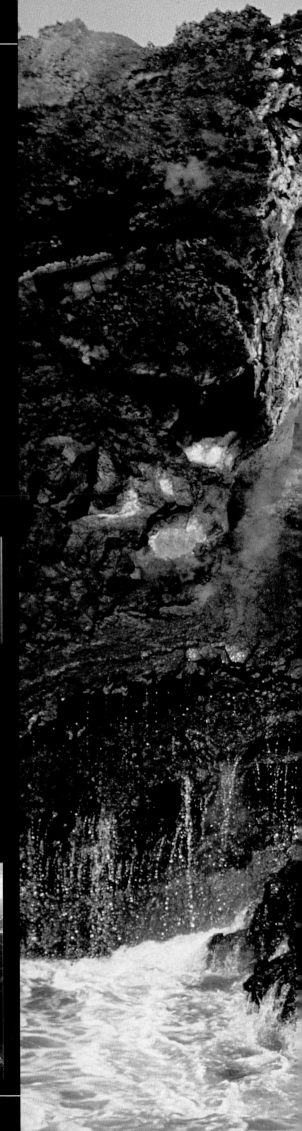

THERE ARE MANY ISLANDS THROUGHOUT the world's oceans, but the greatest number occurs in areas where there is a lot of volcanic activity. Some islands take millions of years to form. Parts of continents sink slowly beneath the sea, leaving the tops of mountains exposed above the water. In contrast, volcanic islands can appear almost overnight – and can also disappear just as quickly. The volcanic island of Krakatoa, in Indonesia, literally blew apart in 1883 – but since then the island has been slowly building up again.

GOD OF FIRE

On November 15, 1963, the island of Surtsey suddenly came up from the sea south of Iceland. An underwater volcano had erupted from the mid-Atlantic ridge, which comes near to the surface in Iceland. Within a few days, the new island was 197 ft (60 m) high and more than 0.3 miles (0.5 km) long.

Surtsey is named after the Old Norse god of fire, Surtur. Seawater poured onto boiling lava as Surtsey was born, and huge clouds of steam and ash rose high into the air.

DRIFTING IN

A new island formed in the middle of the ocean will not remain barren and lifeless for long. The first creatures to arrive will be flying insects and birds. Drifting logs bring in crabs, snails, and even lizards. "Sea beans" from tropical trees can drift thousands of miles to Europe and will still sprout, despite such a long journey!

Coconuts will last for about four months in the sea. After that they start to rot.

CHANGING SHORES

In 1964, a huge earthquake shook the Pacific coast of Alaska. Buildings collapsed, landslides swept roads away, and huge waves battered the coast. Some parts of the coast were lifted up while others sank by several feet. Villages once safe from the sea were now flooded at each high tide, while others found that their boats became stranded well above the new seashore.

Land that was previously under the sea was pushed up by the earthquake to form a wide coastal platform.

Fernandina is the most recently formed of the Galápagos Islands and its volcano, called La Cumbre, is the most active in the entire region. Volcanic eruptions may occur on Fernandina as often as every few years.

FIRE AND WATER

Long after they have been formed, volcanic islands can change in shape and size. This photograph (left) shows lava pouring into the sea from a volcanic eruption on the Galápagos island of Fernandina, in 1995. Once it cools, new ground like this will become a home for many creatures – including humans. The Japanese volcanic island of Miyake-Jima, pictured below, is inhabited by 3,800 people.

The island of Miyake-Jima is dominated by a volcano called Mount Oyama, which is 2,700 ft (820 m) high. This 3-D image of the island was generated using data from a US Space Shuttle mission.

33

ISLAND REFUGE

IN THE VAST EXPANSES OF the open ocean, islands are like desert oases where life can settle and grow. When an island is first formed, it may be colonized by floating plants and seeds, flying insects and birds, and by marine larvae brought to shore by the ocean currents. Fewer creatures will reach isolated islands that are situated far away from reefs, land, or other islands.

A model of the now extinct dodo (Raphus cucullatus)

Cactus ground finch on Plaza Island, Galápagos

OLD SPECIES, NEW SPECIES

There were no predators on the island of Mauritius before people arrived. The flightless dodo was totally unafraid and was soon hunted to extinction. When the remote Galápagos Islands were formed, flocks of finches were blown there by storms. These birds evolved to suit the particular conditions on each island. Each island now has its own specific species.

Komodo dragons grow to between 6.5 ft and 9.75 ft (2 m and 3 m) in length.

LIZARD AT LARGE

Small islands can be home to some very large animals. On a few small islands in Indonesia, you can meet the world's heaviest lizard, the Komodo dragon (*Varanus komodoensis*). These ferocious predators can weigh more than 155 lb (70 kg) and can run fast enough to kill deer and wild pigs for food. However, their usual tactic is to ambush prey.

These tank-like tracks were made by a female turtle as she dragged herself up the beach.

TURTLE HOMES

This green turtle (below) is digging her nest on a sandy beach in the Philippines. Remote islands provide safe nesting sites with fewer predators to eat the eggs and young. Unfortunately, many nesting beaches have now become tourist resorts. Turtles will travel thousands of miles to reach their traditional nesting sites – often the very same island on which they were born.

EGGS

BIRD CITIES

Many seabirds breed in noisy, densely crowded colonies. In spring, thousands of gannets gather to breed on isolated, rocky islands around Scotland. The colony on Saint Kilda has over 50,000 breeding pairs. They create a spectacular air show while wheeling and plunge-diving to catch sprats and herring to feed to their young.

COCONUT THIEF

The Seychelles are home to one of the strangest of all crabs – the coconut or robber crab (*Birgus latro*). This giant, at 8 in (20 cm) long, has claws strong enough to pinch off your finger. It uses these claws to climb trees and cut open young coconuts.

FROZEN SEAS

THE SOUTHERN OCEAN surrounding Antarctica is surprisingly rich in animal life. In winter, pack ice covers more than half the ocean and air temperatures drop to between -4°F (-20°C) and -22°F (-30°C). But in summer, when the ice retreats, huge numbers of birds, seals, whales, fish, and squid hunt for food in the icy waters. Animals such as sponges, anemones, crabs, and starfish thrive on the seabed, even in winter. Under the cover of ice there are no howling gales, and the water temperature remains between 32°F (0°C) and 28°F (-2°C).

Antarctic pack ice helps to keep the Earth cool by reflecting the Sun's rays back into space.

A giant Antarctic spider out on a hunt

GIANT SPIDERS
Animals living on the Antarctic seabed grow very slowly in the icy-cold water. However, most species live for a long time and grow much bigger than their relatives in warmer waters. The giant Antarctic sea spider in the picture (above) is around the same size as a person's hand. Sea spiders in British waters, for example, only grow to about 0.4 in (1 cm) long.

Icefish have thin, pale blood with no red blood cells, so that the blood can circulate easily in the cold conditions.

ANTIFREEZE
In winter, the water temperature around Antarctica often falls below the freezing point of normal fish blood. Icefish survive these conditions because their blood contains glycoprotein. This substance freezes at a lower temperature than water, so the fishes' blood does not freeze, even if trapped in ice. The antifreeze used in car radiators works in the same way.

Adelie penguins spend the winter on the Antarctic pack ice. This one is hesitating before taking a dive into the water, aware that a leopard seal might be lying in wait for it.

THE EMPERORS

Emperor penguins are bigger than any other seabird. They live in huge colonies on the pack ice that surrounds Antarctica. Their large size helps them to survive the hurricane-force winds and temperatures that can drop to as low as -22°F (-30°C) in winter. They can dive down to depths of 650 ft (200 m) or more, and stay down for about 20 minutes while they hunt for fish.

ICY TOMB

The underside of the winter pack ice is riddled with small channels filled with microscopic plants called algae. These give the ice an eerie green color. In spring, when the ice melts, the algae are released and quickly multiply. The algae are eaten by tiny shrimps called krill, which also breed rapidly. This wealth of food is the reason that so many birds, seals, whales, and fish can live in these icy waters.

Starfish gather below seal breathing holes to feed on the seals' feces (deposits of solid waste).

SEALED IN

The leopard seal is a ferocious predator. It is fast and agile underwater and can even outmaneuver a penguin. The seal uses up a lot of energy while chasing its prey, but uses an extra-thick layer of fat, called blubber, to store up energy and keep warm. Young leopard seals mostly eat krill – a tiny shrimp that is also the main food source of the great blue whale.

Although only about 2 in (5 cm) long, krill (Euphausia superba) occur in swarms that may be thousands of feet across, and which could contain several million tons of these tiny shrimps.

KRILL

An Antarctic sea urchin (Sterechinus neumayeri) grazing on the seabed

MARINE MIGRATIONS

IN 1969–70, SIDNEY GENDERS ROWED 3,800 miles (6,114 km) across
the Atlantic Ocean in 74 days. Ten years later, Sir Ranulph Fiennes
trekked 1,348 miles (2,170 km) to the South Pole (1979–82). These are
epic voyages, and yet much longer journeys are made by many ocean
animals every year. Some, like the salmon, can navigate so accurately
that they can return from rich feeding grounds in Greenland to the
very same river in Europe where they were born. There, they recognize
the smell of their home waters. Birds, fish, and whales may all be able
to sense the Earth's magnetic field and use it to guide their way. Birds
can also navigate using the Sun and stars. By traveling so far, these
animals can feed in one area but breed in a much safer spot.

*Gray whales were once hunted
almost to extinction. Today,
their numbers have recovered
and boatloads of tourists travel
to watch them instead.*

THE WHALE ROAD

Every year, gray whales travel
from their rich (but icy-cold) feeding
grounds off Alaska to the safe, warm
coastal lagoons of Baja California,
Mexico. Here, they give birth to their
calves after an incredible 6,000-mile
(9,650-km) journey. The calves
are sometimes attacked by killer
whales on their way back north.

INCREDIBLE JOURNEY

European eels swim right across the Atlantic Ocean to the Sargasso Sea, near Bermuda, to lay their eggs. Exhausted, they all die. The eggs hatch into tiny, leaf-shaped *leptocephalus* larvae. These drift back to Europe, pushed along by the ocean currents.

The Arctic tern always migrates over the ocean so that it can feed on small fish during its long journeys.

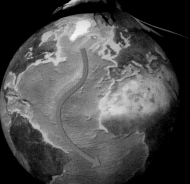

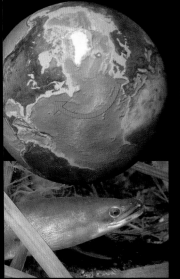

European eel (Anguilla anguilla) *spend up to 20 years in fresh (not salt) water before setting out on its ocean journey to breed.*

ARCTIC TO ANTARCTIC

Arctic terns travel up to 21,750 miles (35,000 km) a year. They nest in summer near to the Arctic Circle. Then, as winter approaches, they fly south to Africa, Australia, and the Antarctic where it will be summer.

MAGNETIC NOSE

Blue sharks travel in a loop around the North Atlantic. They go clockwise with the ocean currents to Europe, Africa, then back across to the Caribbean. They may find their way using a built-in "compass" that detects changes in the Earth's magnetic field.

The blue shark (Prionace glauca) *was once very common, but is now endangered due to overfishing.*

TURTLE TRIPS

Marine turtles roam the oceans, but when it is time to lay eggs many return to the beach where they hatched. Atlantic ridley turtles all return to a few remote beaches in the Gulf of Mexico – once in their thousands, but now only a few are left.

These Atlantic ridley turtles (Lepidochelys kempii) *are coming ashore to lay eggs on a Costa Rican beach.*

LOBSTER LINE

Tropical spiny lobsters (*Panulirus argus*) spend most of their time hiding in rocky crevices with only their long antennae sticking out. So divers are often very surprised to see long lines of them marching purposefully across the seabed. Each year, the lobsters walk to special areas, close inshore, where they lay their eggs. Afterward, they walk back again.

PERFECT BALANCE

LIFE ON EARTH AND IN OUR OCEANS depends on plants. Without them, animals would not exist. Powered by sunlight, plants make their own food by changing water and carbon dioxide gas into sugar and starch – a process known as photosynthesis. Animals eat plants, but they also breathe out carbon dioxide and produce manure that provides nutrients for the plants. In the ocean there is only enough light for seaweeds and sea grasses to grow in shallow water around the ocean edges. The rest of the ocean's plant life consists of billions and billions of tons of phytoplankton – the microscopically small plants that float in the sunlit waters near to the surface.

NO CHAIN
The basking shark (*Cetorhinus maximus*) is found in cool seas. It can grow to up to 33 ft (10 m) long, which makes it the second-largest fish in the ocean. (The whale shark is the biggest.) In spite of its great size, this fish feeds entirely on plankton. Most other sharks are predators at the top of the food chain. Using its huge, gaping mouth, the basking shark can filter many gallons of seawater every hour.

Sharks are top predators. Large hunting species, such as great white sharks, can eat dolphins and seals as well as fish. Bottlenose dolphins eat large numbers of fish that live near the seabed, including cod.

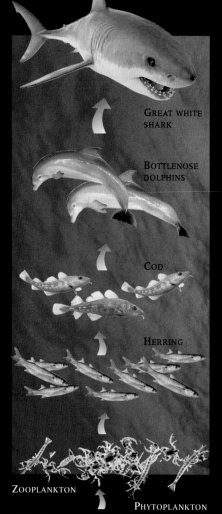

GREAT WHITE SHARK

BOTTLENOSE DOLPHINS

COD

HERRING

ZOOPLANKTON

PHYTOPLANKTON

OCEAN FOOD CHAINS
Most large animals cannot eat plant plankton directly. Instead, the plant plankton (phytoplankton) is "grazed" by tiny animals (zooplankton). These in turn are eaten by small fish, which are eaten by bigger fish, and so on. This system is called a food chain. However, most animals eat a variety of different creatures. They are, therefore, part of a more complex system, known as a food "web."

Herring and sprat are "plankton pickers" that eat the larger zooplankton animals. Herring and sprat are eaten by larger fish such as cod. Cod also eat many other marine creatures and are part of an extensive food web.

Zooplankton consists of animals like copepods, which spend all their life in the plankton, plus the larvae (young) of bottom-dwelling animals such as crabs.

A scanning electron microscope photograph (left) of diatoms, one of the most common types of plant plankton.

BALANCED
Giant tube worms (*Riftia pachyptila*), as tall as a person, live around deepsea volcanic vents. They have no mouth or gut and thus cannot feed. Instead, the worms absorb chemicals from the hot vent water. Bacteria that live inside the worms' bodies use the chemicals to make food for themselves, and also for the worms – a perfectly balanced system.

The worms' bright red gills stick out from their hard, white tubes.

KING RAY

Tropical manta rays (*Manta birostris*) used to have a fearsome reputation – the result of their huge size, strange-looking "horns," and their unnerving habit of jumping up out of the water. They were given the name "devilfish" and were believed to be as dangerous as sharks. When scuba diving began, divers soon found that these graceful animals were so docile they could be stroked. Like basking sharks and whale sharks, these giants only eat plankton and use their "horns" to funnel plankton-rich water into their mouths.

UNBALANCED

California is famous for its beautiful underwater forests of giant kelp seaweeds. Unfortunately, armies of sea urchins are damaging some forests, eating every plant in their path. Humans have broken the delicate food chain by overfishing sheephead fish and, in the past, by hunting sea otters. Sheephead fish and sea otters both eat sea urchins. Without them, the urchins are taking over!

PARTNERS AND PARASITES

FINDING A SAFE HOME IN THE SEA is a problem faced by many defenseless, bite-sized animals such as juvenile fish, shrimps, and small crabs. One ingenious solution involves living with a partner, who acts as a bodyguard. A favorite choice on coral reefs is the giant sea anemone, because it has powerful stinging tentacles. Anemonefish live with these anemones and wear a special coat of slimy mucus that prevents them from being stung. In return for this service, these small fish serve as housekeepers, removing debris in and around the anemone.

Here, a large grouper is having bits of food and debris removed from between its teeth by a hardworking cleaner wrasse.

The clownfish (Amphiprion cellaris), a type of anemonefish, always remains close to its chosen anemone and sleeps deep within the tentacles at night.

CLEANER AT WORK

Just as animals such as rabbits and hedgehogs harbor fleas, many coral reef fish suffer from tiny, shrimplike skin parasites. When these become too troublesome, the fish go for a wash and combing. Certain small fish and shrimps get their food by eating these parasites along with dead skin and scales.

[CU]RTAIN OF DEATH

[Jel]lyfish have some of the most
[po]werful stings of all animals, and
[lar]ge ones can kill and eat fish. Most
[pr]edators therefore steer well clear
[of] them. Some baby fish have learned
[to] take advantage of this by hiding
[am]ong the trailing net of a jellyfish's
[te]ntacles. Out in the open ocean, where
[th]e jellies drift, there is little other cover.
[Slip]ping easily between the tentacles,
[th]ese juvenile fish come to no harm.

LION'S MANE
JELLYFISH

*[...] juvenile jackfish hide among the
[dead]ly tentacles of a giant pelagic
[jelly]fish (Chrysaora achlyos).*

CLOWNFISH WITH LARGE
SEA ANEMONES

HITCHING A RIDE

Some animal partnerships involve getting
a free ride and perhaps sharing the host's
meals. This rather one-sided relationship
suits the remora, a small fish that clings
onto sharks, turtles, and whales. The
remora can swim by itself and often
changes partners. Anemones remain
with their hermit crab hosts until
the crab "relocates" and finds
a bigger shell.

*This closed-up
sea anemone
(Calliactis
parasitica) is
perched on a
hermit crab shell.*

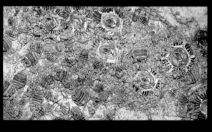

*Close-up of
barnacles and lice
attached to a gray
whale. Barnacles
often settle on
the thick skin
of whales.*

*Two remoras,
also known as
"shark suckers"
(Echeneis
naucrates),
are hitching
a free ride on a
loggerhead turtle
(Caretta caretta).*

DEADLY FOOD

Some sea slugs – colorful relatives of garden
slugs – are able to eat the stinging tentacles
of anemones and sea firs. Instead of digesting
the stinging cells, they store them in special
feathery extensions on their backs. They use
the stolen stings to ward off attacks by fish. This
rainbow sea slug *Dendronotus iris* (below) has
eaten all the tentacles off a large tube anemone.

SURVIVAL

THERE ARE NEARLY AS MANY DIFFERENT sorts of fish in the ocean as there are land mammals and birds put together – around 14,000 species. Each species is faced with the problem of finding food while, at the same time, trying not to become a meal for something bigger than itself. Many are expertly camouflaged, while others are armed with a supply of weapons that are used either for defense or attack – and sometimes for both. As a result, there are some weird-looking shapes and extraordinary lifestyles in the world of fish.

SLEEPING PARROT

Like their bird namesakes, parrotfish are brightly colored and have their teeth join together into a tough, parrot-like beak. Th spend their days busily scraping and bitin the corals (their food). At night, exhauste all this activity, they go to sleep while we into a rock crevice. Many cover themselv a cocoon of slimy mucus, which prevents predators from sniffing them out.

STAYING PUT

Garden eels survive by retreating deep into their burrows when danger threatens. Large colonies of these strange fish live in sandy areas near to coral reefs. Swaying gracefully from side to side, the eels rise up out of their burrows to feed on passing plankton. They are very sensitive to vibrations and to the noise made by scuba divers' air bubbles. As a result, they are very difficult to photograph underwater.

The spotted garden eel (Heteroconger hassi) lives in the warm waters of the Red Sea and the Indian Ocean.

SELF DEFENCE

When a porcupinefish is out hunting for crabs and snails, it keeps its spines folded back along its body and looks quite harmless – just like an actual porcupine does. If it is attacked, it immediately swallows huge mouthfuls of water and inflates itself into a ball-shape. Surgeonfish defend themselves by extending sharp spines at either side of their tails.

PUFFERFISH

Few predators would dare attack a fully inflated porcupinefish or pufferfish, like this one (above).

LEAFY SEA DRAGON

Long skin tassles help to camouflage this weird relative of the seahorse, which lives among seaweeds.

HAMMERHEAD SHARK

HAMMER-VISION

As well as an excellent sense of smell, sharks have extremely good eyesight. A hammerhead's eyes are at each end of a flattened, hammer-shaped head. The head is kept moving at all times – so that the shark can see in every direction – and is also used as a rudder.

This blenny pretends to be a cleaner fish, ready to remove irritating parasites from larger fish – but instead it darts in and takes a bite out of its surprised target.

FALSE CLEANER BLENNY

SHOCKING TACTICS

The electric ray has a very unusual ability – it can give a diver, fisherman, or predator who touches it a nasty shock! The electric shock is produced in special organs on the ray's "wings." The ray also uses

MARBLED ELECTRIC RAY

this ability to stun or kill fish to eat. It lies quietly in wait on the seabed until a fish swims within reach.

THE KILLERS

WHEN WE THINK OF really dangerous marine creatures, most people would name sharks as the villains. However, while all sharks should be treated with respect, they rarely attack humans. Most other sea creatures that can hurt – or even kill – humans are small and do not look dangerous at all. Jellyfish, sea snakes, and some fish, seashells, and octopuses are armed with a venomous bite or sting. Some use their venom to help capture and subdue their prey, but when they sting or bite us it is because we have accidentally trodden on them or picked them up. They are simply trying to defend themselves.

SEA SNAKES

Sea snakes are found mostly in the warm, tropical waters of the Indian and Pacific oceans. The banded sea krait, *Laticauda colubrina* (right), is often seen on coral reefs by divers and snorkelers. Using its specially flattened tail to swim efficiently from place to place, it hunts for small fish hiding in coral crevices or sandy burrows. A bite from a sea snake can be as deadly as that of a cobra, but most are shy and docile and will not attack humans unless provoked. Most sea snake-related deaths are of fishermen who are bitten by snakes that get tangled up in their nets.

DEADLY BOX

At certain times of the year, many beaches along the northern coast of Australia are closed to swimmers. This region is the haunt of the box jellyfish (*Chironex fleckeri*), one of the most venomous animals in the world. The intensely painful sting of this beautiful creature can kill in just a few minutes. The deadly tentacles hang down in bunches from each corner of the box-shaped top, and survivors often have dramatic scars to remind them of their brush with death.

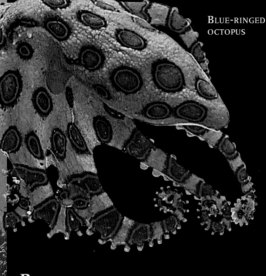

BLUE-RINGED OCTOPUS

...t victims of the blue-
...ed octopus are Australian
...ationers who find the little
...pus in sea shells or under
...s on the seashore.

COLLECTING SHELLS

The beauty of cone shells belies their deadly nature. These tropical shells crawl over coral reefs and shores searching for fish and other prey. They attack by thrusting out a minute "harpoon" on the end of a long proboscis. One stab of venom and it is all over. Not all species are poisonous, but some can kill a person – so these shells should never be handled.

CONE SHELLS

The tiny, poisonous "harpoon" of
a striated cone (Conus striatus)

BLUE-RINGED BITER

Compared with the giant octopus, whose stretched-out arms could envelop a bus, the tiny blue-ringed octopus – often smaller than a human hand – seems quite harmless. Nothing could be further from the truth. Although its bite is painless, it can kill a man in only a few minutes. The victim becomes paralyzed and stops breathing.

LIONFISH

The lionfish
or turkeyfish
(Pterois
volitans) has an
extremely painful
sting, but it is unlikely to
kill a person.

STONEFISH

Stonefish
(Synanceia
species) live in
shallow tropical seas
and are the world's
most venomous fish.

RED TIDES

Not oil or pollution, but billions of tiny, single-celled creatures called *dinoflagellates* have caused this red slick on the sea (below). The presence of sewage in the water has caused a population explosion. *Dinoflagellates* are a type of floating plant plankton that multiply very quickly. Some species are poisonous and humans can become seriously ill after eating shellfish that have been feeding in the area.

SWORD IN THE STONE

Stonefish and lionfish are safe from attack by predators because they have an armory of sharp, poisonous spines in their fins. The flamboyant red and white lionfish is easy to spot; its colors warn us to stay away. In contrast, the stonefish is a master of disguise. Treading on a stonefish may be the last thing you do, since a sting from its swordlike spines can be fatal.

Dinoflagellates *come in*
many intricate shapes and not
all of them produce poisons.

47

GOING DOWN

Today's scuba-diving equipment is light and easy to use – and also colorful! With the correct training, children as young as 12 years old can now learn to dive safely, carrying their air supply in a cylinder mounted on their backs. The normal depth limit for a scuba diver (breathing air) is around 164 ft (50 m). By using special vehicles and equipment, scientists, explorers – and even film crews – can now go beyond this limit and visit all except the very deepest parts of the oceans.

UNDERWATER PHOTOGRAPHY

The equipment needed to make professional underwater films is still quite large and expensive. However, there is now a huge range of relatively inexpensive underwater cameras available for ordinary divers to use. Tourists can even buy disposable underwater cameras. Louis Boutan, who took the first underwater photographs in 1893, would have been amazed by these new gadgets.

This diver is doing some underwater filming using a Betacam SP video camera.

A demand valve, or "regulator," controls the flow of air from the cyclinder to the diver, providing air whenever the diver sucks on the mouthpiece.

HS1200
PRESSURE
SUIT

HS2000
PRESSURE
SUIT

PRESSURE SUITS

Imagine walking around on the seabed in your own personal made-to-measure submarine! That is what it is like to wear a pressure suit. The pressure inside the tough, hard suit is kept the same as it is at the surface of the ocean. This means that the diver is not crushed by the much higher pressure at greater depths.

The hydraulic pincers on these pressure suits act as hands.

The diver in this HS2000 suit can work as deep as 1,640 ft (500 m) for approximately six to eight hours.

SUBMERSIBLES

Submersibles are like miniature submarines. They are mainly used to take research scientists into the deep sea, but some now carry tourists. The people on board a submersible are protected inside a strong, pressure-resistant capsule. The hull is filled with a lightweight material called syntactic foam, which helps it to float.

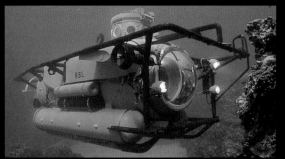

The RSL submersible has a transparent viewing sphere made of thick acrylic plastic. This gives its passengers an excellent view. However, it can only go down to around 800 ft (244 m).

REMOTELY OPERATED VEHICLES (ROVS)

ROVs are unmanned craft used to explore, film, measure, and collect samples underwater. They are connected to a mother ship by long cables. Cameras transmit images to operators on the ship, who can steer the vehicle as though they were in it. Satellite links allow scientists to follow the action as it happens, via the Internet.

Solo (above) is an ROV used for pipeline surveys and other underwater work in the North Sea oil fields.

UNDERWATER HOTELS

As with space tourism, underwater vacations are now a possibility. Tourist submarines operate in the Caribbean, and in Florida, guests can stay in a hotel called *Jules' Undersea Lodge*. The record for living continuously underwater is 69 days and 19 minutes.

MARINE ARCHAEOLOGY

THE SEA RUSTS METAL, ROTS WOOD, and breaks up glass, but it can also preserve shipwrecks and artifacts for many centuries by burying them under shifting sand and mud. Such "time capsules" are a treasure trove of information for historians and archaeologists. Others hunt for wrecks in the hope of finding precious treasure – coins, gold, valuable china, and even wine! Few succeed, but in 1985, an American named Mel Fisher found a Spanish wreck off the coast of Florida that sank in 1622, carrying 40 tons (40.6 tonnes) of gold, silver, and emeralds.

The Sankisan Maru under attack in Pearl Harbor, 1944

THE MARY ROSE

On October 11, 1982, King Henry VIII's flagship, the *Mary Rose*, saw the light of day for the first time in 437 years. Her hull was raised to the surface and is now in a museum at the Royal Naval base in Portsmouth, England (UK). Divers and archaeologists spent ten years carefully measuring, recording, and excavating the ship before she was raised. They recovered thousands of objects, from shoes and hair combs to bows and arrows.

Wreck of the Kasi Maru, New Georgia, Solomon Islands

NEW FROM OLD

During World War II, many ships and airplanes were sunk. While this was a tragic end for many brave servicemen, it was the start of a new life for the wrecks. Soon after they sank, plants and animals quickly began to settle on the Japanese freighters shown above. In the tropics, a rusting hulk can transform into a living, artificial reef in a matter of months.

The picture to the right shows the Mary Rose being sprayed with preserving chemicals in the museum.

MODEL OF THE *MARY ROSE*

PEWTER JUG FROM THE *MARY ROSE*

BURIED AT SEA

Walk along the shore at Lyme Regis in Dorset, England, and you will be walking over millions of years of history. The cliffs and shores there are full of the fossilized remains of ancient animals, such as the ammonite shown in the picture below. When it died, the ammonite was first buried in silt at the bottom of the ocean and later turned to stone through a complex chemical process.

TREASURE HUNTERS

Every shipwreck is owned by somebody. Ancient wrecks are usually the property of the government of a country. Most countries have rules about how much "treasure" can be kept by the finder. Salvage companies usually make a deal with the wreck owner or with the government.

This ammonite fossil is about 200 million years old.

ROMAN JAR COVERED IN SEA CREATURES

18TH CENTURY GOLD DOUBLOONS (SPANISH COINS)

The remains of this US fighter plane, a Grumman F6F-3 "Hellcat," has attracted a variety of reef fish and is of great interest to divers and marine historians.

HARVEST FROM THE SEA

PEOPLE THE WORLD OVER HAVE ALWAYS harvested what they need from the sea, and many people in poor, coastal regions depend entirely on fishing for their food and livelihood. In Southeast Asia, many such coastal communities rely on aquaculture – the "farming" of the sea. Seaweed, giant clams, oysters, tiger prawns, and milkfish are just some of the famers' "crops." The Bajau Laut, or sea gypsies, in Malaysia spend their entire lives out at sea on their boats. Usually, they only come ashore to bury their dead.

A WAY OF LIFE

Fishing is also a way of life for thousands of people in developed regions such as Europe and the US. The photograph (above) shows a European double-beamed shrimp trawler collecting its catch. Many families have been fishing for generations, but overfishing has drastically reduced fish stocks throughout the oceans. In some places, whole communities have stopped fishing. In the future, fish farms and indoor hatcheries on land may become the main source for popular fish such as cod.

MUSSELS   WINKLES   COCKLES

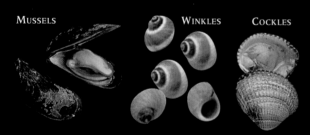

As long as they are adequately washed, hand-collected shellfish can provide an excellent free meal.

"ALIVE, ALIVE-OH!"

Cockles, mussels, and periwinkles can easily be collected on shores around Europe. Hand-collecting causes few problems for worldwide stocks, but in areas where commercial machines – such as cockle dredgers – are used, these shellfish soon become scarce.

MARINE MEDICINES

Many colorful sponges grow on coral reefs around the world. Some produce powerful chemicals that prevent other creatures from growing over them. Scientists have found that some of these chemicals can be used to combat illnesses such as malaria and cancer. Whenever a useful sponge chemical is discovered, scientists try to reproduce it in the laboratory to save collecting up too many wild sponges.

An azure vase sponge (right) from the Caribbean. New sponge species are discovered on coral reefs every year.

SEAWEED STRINGS

Seaweed is farmed in many developing countries in tropical parts of the world, and provides an income for local families. It can be sold as food, fertilizer, and as an ingredient for other products Small pieces of seaweed are tied onto ropes and staked out in the sea (right), often with plastic bottles attached to the ropes as floats. When it has grown big enough, the seaweed is collected

STRING OF PEARLS

Pearls are one of the most valuable natural products found in the sea. When an oyster gets a bit of irritating material inside its shell, it covers it with shiny, smooth layers of a precious material called mother-of-pearl. Pearl farmers in the South Pacific hang oysters on ropes and slip small pieces of broken shell into them so that they make pearls.

A diver is inspecting his pearl oysters to check that they are healthy, and that the ropes are not frayed or damaged.

Many different species of oysters and mussels can produce pearls, but they are not always as perfectly formed as these ones (above right).

SALMON FARMING

In northern Europe, salmon can be bought in most supermarkets. Most of it now comes not from wild-caught stocks, but from Scottish and Norwegian fish farms. The fish are grown in suspended pens and, as in the photograph (left), are fed pellets made from fish meal

A FARMED
SALMON

IMPACT ON THE OCEANS

PEOPLE ONCE THOUGHT THAT THE OCEANS were so vast that nothing we did could ever affect them. Unfortunately, this is no longer true. Modern technology, huge increases in the world's population, and a lack of management have resulted in some serious problems. Today, overfishing is one of the most serious. Catching large numbers of a few species upsets the delicate balance of nature. Other serious problems include pollution from poorly treated sewage, effluents from oil spills, litter, and the destruction of coral reefs. These problems can be solved – but only if nations and governments work together.

A humpback whale lifts its huge tail fluke before diving in

Spermaceti oil from sperm whales was used as a lubricant and for making candles.

IN FOR THE KRILL

Most countries have banned commercial whaling, and a large part of the Southern Ocean around Antarctica is now a whale sactuary. But Japan and Norway still catch whales legally. Krill, the tiny shrimps on which many whales feed, is now harvested from the Southern Ocean – a new threat to the few remaining whales

OVERFISHING

Cod was once the most plentiful fish the North Atlantic. It was so commo that whole communities depended on it for a living. Today, there are far fewer, due to modern fishing methoc that track where the fish are and tra them up in huge quantities. Fishing cod has now been stopped or restrict in some areas, which should allow their numbers to increase.

Although cod can live for at least 20 (and possibly 30) years, there are now virtually no cod in the

ARCTIC IMPROVEMENTS

The inhospitable Arctic Ocean is perhaps the least exploited ocean region, mainly because it is so difficult to work there. In the 1970s and 1980s, thousands of baby harp seals were killed each year for their white fur – but no longer. Inuit people hunt walruses and seals, but they only take what they need for food and clothing.

CORAL MINING

Throughout the Indian Ocean, there are many small island nations such as the Maldives. Island resorts are becoming popular with tourists who want to visit the coral reefs and beautiful beaches. Many hotels and jetties used by these tourists are built using coral rock mined from the reefs, which are damaged as a result.

This small wooden house by the sea in Indonesia is protected by a wall built from coral blocks.

e depths. Individual whales can be recognized from markings on their tails.

SPILLS

spills occur in oceans and seas ughout the world. They are mainly ed by oil tankers that run aground. siderable damage can occur when oil goes ashore, especially if there major seabird or seal colonies by. Smaller – and more frequent lls from ships illegally washing heir tanks can be just as damaging arine life. Out at sea, spills can eated with detergents – but many e-dwelling animals are sensitive ese chemicals.

An oil tanker spilling oil at Pearl Harbor, Oahu, Hawaii

This auk is covered in oil from the 1996 Sea Empress disaster in Wales, UK. Most oiled birds die even if they are cleaned up.

REMOTE SENSING

UNDERSTANDING HOW THE OCEANS work is the job of oceanographers. These scientists used to spend many weeks at sea measuring water temperature, currents, waves, and water clarity. Nowadays, satellites can obtain information about the sea by measuring electromagnetic radiation. The data is sent to powerful computers that convert the readings into temperature, color, wave height, and current speed information.

EUROPEAN REMOTE-SENSING SATELLITE (*ERS-1*)

ERS-1 *was launched into orbit by the* Ariane 4 *rocket on July 17, 1991.*

OCEANOGRAPHIC SURVEYS

The *ERS-1* satellite orbits Earth and is used to collect data on coastlines, oceans, and polar ice. Scientists around the world are using it to study climate change. Sensors on the satellite detect microwaves, which can pass through clouds, unlike the visible light needed to take photographs.

CURRENTLY WARM

Sea surface temperatures are measured by satellite sensors that detect infrared radiation. This image, from the *NOAA 11* satellite, shows the origin of the Gulf Stream – a current that carries warm water from around Florida to the shores of Britain. Without it, Britain would have a climate as cold as Greenland. Red and yellow indicate warm water. Blue and gray show cool water.

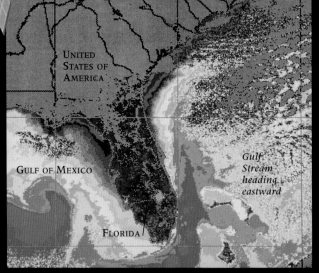

UNITED STATES OF AMERICA

GULF OF MEXICO

Gulf Stream heading eastward

FLORIDA

JAPANESE TUNA

TUNA TROUBLE

Modern fishing boats make full use of satellite technology, computers, and sonar to help them locate and catch fish shoals. With sonar, pulses of sound are sent down into the water and "bounce" back if they hit shoals of fish. The time taken for echoes to return is measured and these readings help to pinpoint large shoals of fish, worthy of pursuit. Valuable tuna shoals are also "spotted" by light aircraft. Sadly, these methods are so efficient that some species, such as bluefin tuna, are becoming very scarce.

A shark is caught using a baited line and bro safely aboard the ship in a netted "hammock

Shallow sandbanks show up as
pale blue areas, while deep water
channels or lagoons are dark blue.

BIRD'S EYE VIEWS

erial photographs can be used to
urvey coastlines and coral reefs and
o monitor the effects of oil spills.
hotographs taken from airplanes
ve a closer view, while satellites
an cover very large areas. This
hotograph shows Kayangel Atoll,
 ring of coral reefs (an atoll) in the
acific Ocean. By repeating the survey
 a later date, changes in the shifting
ndbanks – and the vegetation trying
 grow on them – can be documented.

The buildup of sand, and
other sediments, drifting
across the reef eventually
causes sandy islands to
form. Wind-borne plant
seeds bring new vegetation
to these young islands.

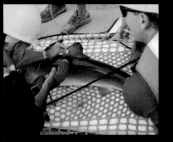

e tag is quickly attached to the
ark's dorsal fin using a special tool.

13095

Once the satellite tag has
been attached, the tag's
number is recorded and
the shark is carefully
returned to the sea.

This is an
example of the
sort of tag used to track
sharks and other large
marine animals.

SATELLITE TRACKING

Satellite tags are used to track the
movements of large animals such as
sharks, whales, and turtles. The tags record
where the animal is and transmit the data
to a satellite when the animal is on the
surface. By following the movements of
endangered species, such as blue whales
and bluefin tuna, scientists will be able
to make plans to protect these animals.

FLUID WORLD

WHEN THE ENGINEER NIKOLAUS OTTO DEVISED the first four-stroke internal combustion engine, in 1876, he could never have dreamed that one day his invention would affect our climate and our oceans. Cars use engines based on his design and each day, tens of millions of them spit out carbon dioxide gas in their exhaust fumes. This gas traps the Sun's heat and is one of the causes of "global warming." Some scientists predict that global warming will cause sea levels to rise – firstly because the polar ice will melt, and secondly because warm water takes up more space than cold water does.

MELTING ICE
Nobody can yet say for sure whether global warming is affecting the ice caps in the Arctic and Antarctic. However, there are some worrying signs. Glaciers such as the Hubbard Glacier in Alaska (left) are retreating and growing smaller, iceberg numbers have increased, and temperatures in the Antarctic are rising.

EL NIÑO
Every few years, changes in wind patterns and water currents in the Pacific Ocean cause an event called *El Niño*. Unusually warm water moves eastward toward South America. This causes heavy rain, violent storms, and cuts off the food supply for fish such as anchovies.

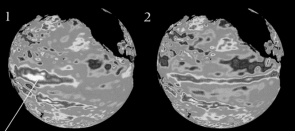

1   2

This computer-enhanced satellite image, taken on April 25, 1997, shows an area of unusually warm water – the start of an El Niño event. Global warming could be making El Niño *events worse.*

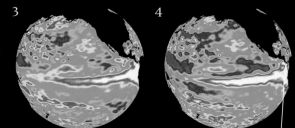

3   4

By September 5, 1997, the warm water has reached the coast of Peru, where the anchovy population is affected. Without the anchovies, many birds die and fishermen face great hardship.

NOT SO SILENT WORLD
The famous diver Jacques Cousteau gave the title *Silent World* to his book about the oceans. Sadly, our seas are no longer silent places. Loud noises from oil exploration, commercial shipping, scientific experiments, and naval exercises may be confusing whales and dolphins. This could be one reason that these animals sometimes get stranded on the shore.

Bottlenose dolphin (Tursiops truncatus)

"Alternative," or "renewable," energy sources – such as wind power – do not produce carbon dioxide or other wastes. However, they are not yet efficient or cheap enough to completely replace fossil fuels.

CLEAN ENERGY
Burning oil, coal, and other "fossil fuels" in power stations releases carbon dioxide into the atmosphere, which adds to global warming. This is why "clean" ways of making electricity are being developed, using the power of the wind, Sun, and tides. This picture shows the Livermore Wind Farm in California.

TIDAL POWER
This tidal barrage, built across the French River Rance, generates power from every tide. The tide is allowed to swirl in through the sluice gates to fill the river estuary. The gates are then closed, as the tide starts to fall, and the water is released through 24 turbines, which generate approximately 240 million watts of electricity.

Tidal barrages only work where there are big tides. The tidal range at this dam reaches 44 ft (13.5 m). The barrage is 2,500 ft (750 m) long and creates an artificial lake 8.5 sq miles (22 sq km) in area.

...uge chunks of ...e are falling from ...e front edge of ...e glacier, where ...reaches the sea.

TIDES OF CHANGE

THERE IS NO DOUBT THAT OUR WORLD and its oceans face many problems. We hear on the news of global warming, overfishing, and massive oil spills. Government action is needed to tackle these issues, but individuals can take action, too. For example, if tourists refuse to buy souvenirs such as shark jaws and turtle shells, fishermen will stop catching the animals. Sharks in popular diving spots are now worth much more alive than dead because diving tourists will pay to see them.

MARINE ALIENS

When ships sail around the world's oceans, they sometimes carry "stowaway" plants and animals on their hulls or among their cargo. Japweed (*Sargassum muticum*) came to the UK from Japan. It now grows all along the south coast of England and getting rid of the stuff has proven impossible.

Once plentiful, Kemp's ridley sea turtles are now the most endangered of all turtle species. Sometimes, ocean currents carry young ones over to Europe from the US.

FISHING FOR PUFFINS

ATLANTIC PUFFIN
(*FRATERCULA ARCTICA*)

The Shetland Islands, off northern Scotland, are home to many thousands of puffins that nest in cliff-top burrows. In the 1980s, the numbers of puffins fell dramatically. Fishing boats had caught so many sand eels that few were left for the puffins to feed their chicks.

Puffins rely on a good supply of sand eels to feed to their chicks. Recent fishing restrictions have made the eels more plentiful.

BRENT SPAR

The *Brent Spar* was a massive, 3,900-to (4,000-tonne) Nort Sea oil platform. W it was no longer nee the owners planne sink it into the ocea depths. There follo a public outcry ove contamination this would cause, and it eventually dismant onshore in spite of cost. Ordinary peor had won the day

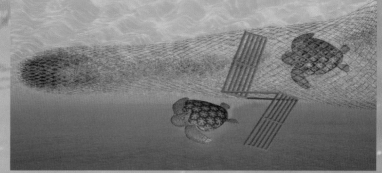

TURTLE EXCLUSION DEVICE (TED)

SHRIMPS IN, TURTLES OUT

Kemp's ridley turtles are the rarest of the six species of turtle found in our oceans. In the Gulf of Mexico, many turtles get caught in nets towed by fishing boats that are trawling for shrimps. The turtles usually drown because they cannot get to the surface to breathe. Luckily, scientists have developed nets with special "escape hatches" (above) that allow the turtles to get out without losing the shrimp catch.

KEMP'S RIDLEY SEA TURTLE
(*LEPIDOCHELYS KEMPII*)

This snorkeler is swimming with fish in a marine reserve area in Belize, Central America.

THE PLASTIC PERIL

Litter on beaches is a big problem. It comes from ships, fishing boats, tourists, and sewers. Plastic is especially dangerous as it lasts a long time and can injure or kill wildlife. Dumping plastic waste from ships is banned in many sea areas but the problem remains. Volunteers sometimes help out in organized beach "cleanups."

RINE RESERVES

re are many marine parks and reserves around world where fishing and collecting are banned or ricted. Marine reserves provide a safe haven for fish other ocean creatures. As in the picture (above), fish can become very tame. However, the amount cean that can be protected in this way is tiny.

OCEAN DATA

SEA STATE: THE BEAUFORT SCALE (simplified)

Force	Wind speed (knots)	Descriptive term	Sea state	Probable wave height (feet)
0	< 1	Calm	Sea like a mirror	0.0 ft (0.0 m)
1	1–3	Light air	Ripples with the appearance of scales	0.3 ft (0.1 m)
2	4–6	Light breeze	Small wavelets	0.7 ft (0.2 m)
3	7–10	Gentle breeze	Large wavelets; crests begin to break	2.0 ft (0.6 m)
4	11–16	Moderate breeze	Small waves becoming longer; fairly frequent "white horses" (white-topped waves)	3.3 ft (1.0 m)
5	17–21	Fresh breeze	Moderate waves; many white horses	6.6 ft (2.0 m)
6	22–27	Strong breeze	Large waves; white horses everywhere; probably some spray	9.8 ft (3.0 m)
7	28–33	Near gale	Sea heaps up; white foam from breaking waves begins to be blown in streaks along the direction of the wind	13.0 ft (4.0 m)
8	34–40	Gale	Moderately high, long waves; foam from crests is blown in well-marked streaks along direction of wind	18.0 ft (5.5 m)
9	41–47	Strong gale	High waves; dense streaks of foam along direction of wind; crests of waves begin to topple, tumble, and roll over	23.0 ft (7.0 m)
10	48–55	Storm	Very high waves with long, overhanging crests; the resulting foam is blown in dense, white streaks along direction of wind; surface takes on a white appearance; tumbling of the sea becomes very heavy and shock-like	29.5 ft (9.0 m)
11	56–63	Violent storm	Exceptionally high waves; sea completely covered with long, white patches of foam lying along direction of wind; everywhere the edges of the wave crests are blown into froth; visibility affected	37.7 ft (11.5 m)
12	64 +	Hurricane	Air filled with foam and spray; sea completely white with driving spray; visibility very seriously affected	46.0 ft (14.0 m)

OCEAN RECORDS

Highest storm wave In 1933, an American ship, the *USS Ramapo*, encountered a terrible storm on its way from Manila, Philippines, to San Diego. One of the crew measured a wave 112 ft (34 m) high.

Highest recorded wave The greatest wave ever recorded was created by a massive landslide in an inlet in Alaska (July 9, 1958). The falling rock caused a wave to surge up the opposite side of the bay, which reached a height of 1,740 ft (530 m).

Deepest part of the ocean The Challenger Deep in the Mariana Trench, between Japan and Papua New Guinea, has a maximum recorded depth of 36,198 ft (11,033 m).

Deepest manned craft On January 23, 1960, the bathyscape *Trieste* descended to a depth of 35,820 ft (10,918 m) in the Challenger Deep with two people on board. The record still stands.

Worst whirlpools The Malstrøm is a famous whirlpool that forms when strong tides run through narrow passages between the Lofotodden Islands off Norway's rugged west coast.

Biggest tides (and tidal range) The difference in height between high and low water in the Bay of Fundy, in Canada, is 53.5 ft (16 m).

Most dramatic tidal bore In the Qiantang River estuary, in China, the incoming tide funnels seawater up the river as a fast wave called the *Black Dragon*, which reaches heights of up to 30 ft (9 m).

Highest submarine mountain The top of Mo Kea in the Pacific Ocean is 33,476 ft (10,203 m) above the seafloor. It is significantly higher than Mount Everest, the tallest mountain on land, which is 29,037 ft (8,850 m) tall.

MARINE WILDLIFE RECORDS

Biggest marine animal Blue whale. Largest recorded length: 102 ft (31 m). Largest recorded weight: 193 tons (196 tonnes). Bigger ones may exist.

Biggest invertebrate Giant squid. Largest known specimen: 55 ft (16.8 m) long. Much larger examples may exist.

Biggest jellyfish Lion's mane jellyfish (*Cyanea capillata*). Bell diameter: 7.5 ft (2.3 m). Tentacle length: 120 ft (36.5 m).

Smallest vertebrate Dwarf goby fish. Adults average 0.35 in (8.8 mm) long.

Tallest seaweed Giant kelp (*Macrocystis*) can reach nearly 197 ft (60 m) tall – see pages 22-23.

Longest migration (swimming) Gray whale. A roundtrip of 12,400 miles (20,000 km) – see page 38.

Most dangerous vertebrate Great white shark. Grows to at least 21 ft (6.5 m) long. Mainly eats seals, sea lions, dolphins, and large fish – see page 40.

Most dangerous invertebrate Box jellyfish (*Chironex fleckeri*). Its sting can kill – see page 46.

Deepest diver Sperm whale. Can probably reach depths of at least 9,800 ft (3,000 m) – see page 7.

Living fossil Coelacanth. This fish belongs to a group that was thought to have been extinct since the Cretaceous Period (135–70 MYA). However, a specimen was caught in 1938.

Loudest sound produced Some baleen whales produce sounds that can travel all the way across entire oceans.

OCEAN MYTHOLOGY

The Kraken Stories about the legendary Kraken came out of Norway in the 12th century. They told of a giant, octopus-like creature that was believed to sink ships. The mythical beast is probably based on the giant squid (see "Marine wildlife records," left).

Sea monsters Sailors used to believe that the sea was filled with deadly sea monsters. Sightings of huge whales probably gave rise to some of these stories.

Mermaids Mermaid legends, from as early as the 8th century BC, refer to creatures with a human, female top half and a scaly, fish tail as a bottom half. Sea cows (dugongs) may be the basis of this myth, although their whiskery faces are not particularly beautiful!

Sea serpents Oarfish have an eel-like body, of up to 23 ft (7 m) long, and a bright red crest along their back. They probably inspired many stories about sea serpents.

Devilfish The huge but harmless manta ray (see page 41) was once thought to be able to drag ships out to sea by their anchor chains.

OCEAN DATA

OCEAN TIMELINE and HISTORY OF MARINE EXPLORATION

EAN TIMELINE:

billion years ago Earth forms

billion years ago The
densation of atmospheric water
es the true oceans to form

0 million years ago Life exists
in the oceans

0 million years ago The age
sh

0–180 million years ago
supercontinent *Pangaea* begins
reak up

0 million years ago The age
eptiles, dinosaurs (on land), and
hyosaurs and plesiosaurs in
ocean

million years ago Primitive
les swim in the oceans

2.5 million years ago Primitive
man beings appear

HISTORY OF EXPLORATION:

• **1831–36** Charles Darwin travels on
his famous voyage on board the *Beagle*,
making observations (regarding wildlife)
that lead to his revolutionary theory of
natural selection

• **1872–76** The voyage of the *HMS
Challenger* – the first comprehensive
oceanographic research expedition

• **1912** The *RMS Titanic* sinks

• **1920** Echo sounding equipment
first used

• **1940s** Aqualung (scuba) equipment
is invented

• **1960** The bathyscape *Trieste* reaches
the deepest part of the ocean

• **1977** Extraordinary animals are found
around deepsea volcanic vents

• **1985–87** The wreck of the *Titanic*
is found and filmed by a submersible

OCEAN FACTS

The amount of water contained by the oceans
is around 326 million cubic miles (1.4 billion cubic km).
The five oceans (biggest to smallest) are the Pacific,
Atlantic, Indian, Southern (Antarctic), and the Arctic.
The Pacific Ocean is the biggest of the five oceans.
It covers an area of more than 63 million square miles
(163 million square km).
Seas of the world Seas are smaller than oceans.
Oceanographers recognize about 54 official seas.
Inland seas Some seas (e.g. Dead Sea, Caspian Sea)
are landlocked and have no connection to the ocean.
Salinity The saltiness (salinity) of the ocean is measured
in parts per thousand (ppt). The average salinity is 35 ppt,
which means 35 units of salt in every 1,000 units of water.
Elements The ocean contains all the known elements,
although some are only present in tiny amounts.
Temperature varies widely in the ocean. It ranges
from 28°F (-2°C) in the Arctic and Southern oceans
to 97°F (36°C), during the summer, in the Arabian Gulf.
Sound travels 4.5 times faster through seawater than it
does through air.

GLOSSARY

ssal plain Broad, flat areas of the ocean
n floor, usually below 12,000 ft (3,650 m).
ssal trench Long, narrow, deep
ression of the deep ocean floor with
tively steep sides.
ae A group of plants that includes
veeds and single-celled, floating plankton.
ll Ring of coral surrounding a lagoon that
ns on the site of a sunken, volcanic island.
hyscape An early type of submarine
nted by Auguste Piccard.
bon dioxide A gas breathed out by living
nisms. Also a byproduct of burning fossil
s, such as gasoline (in cars).
epods Tiny, shrimp-like animals that
part of the ocean's plankton.
oflagellates A group of single-celled
nisms that form part of the plankton.
ne produce poisons that kill sea creatures.
inoderms A group of marine animals
t includes starfish, brittlestars, sea urchins,
cucumbers, and featherstars.
pelagic (sunlit) zone The top open

water zone of the ocean, which runs from
the surface down to about 650 ft (200 m).
Hydrothermal vent A crack in the seabed
where hot water gushes upward, after being
heated by volcanic activity.
Larvae Young stages of an invertebrate
animal (an animal without a backbone),
usually completely different in shape and size
from the adult. Many marine animals produce
floating (planktonic) larvae.
Lithosphere The outer surface part of the
Earth, which includes the outermost part of
the planet's rigid crust.
Luciferin A chemical that gives out light in
bioluminescent animals such as deepsea fish.
Meiofauna Microscopically small animals,
less than 0.02 in (0.5 mm) long, which mainly
live in the spaces between grains of sand.
Mesopelagic (twilight) zone The middle
depths of the open ocean – from
approximately 650 ft (200 m) to 6,500 ft
(2,000 m) in depth – where there is some
light, but not very much.

Oceanography The scientific study
of the ocean, including physical, chemical,
and biological aspects.
Oxygen A gas breathed in or absorbed
by all living creatures for respiration.
Photosynthesis The process by which
plants make their own food, using energy
from sunlight to turn water and carbon
dioxide gas into sugars and oxygen.
Polyps Tiny animals that resemble
anemones. Corals consist of many polyps
joined together in a colony.
Sublittoral zone The area of seabed from
just below the seashore down to a depth
of about 325 ft (100 m).
Zooplankton Tiny, floating animals. Some
spend their whole lives floating, while others
are the larvae of bottom-dwelling creatures
such as snails and crabs.
Zooxanthellae Single-celled plants that live
inside the bodies of corals – plus some sea
anemones – and help to make extra
food for them.

OCEAN WEBSITES

p://www.noaa.gov/
US government's official National Oceanic and Atmospheric
ninistration (NOAA) website. Offers news and educational information.

p://www.jncc.gov.uk/mermaid/
d out about British marine life and habitats. Best navigated with the
stance of an adult.

p://www.bbc.co.uk/nature/blueplanet/
BBC's online guide to the natural history of the oceans.

p://mbgnet.mobot.org/salt/animals/
an animals. Need to find out about a particular marine animal? Just
k on the one you want, and read on. A great help with homework!

p://www.fishbase.org/search.cfm
ormation on almost all species of fish. Photographs help to identify
n species.

p://www.geo.nsf.gov/oce/ocekids.htm/
s web portal has links to lots of very good underwater
loration websites.

http://www.ocean.udel.edu/deepsea/
Voyage to the deep. Plunge into the ocean depths with deep
submersible craft *Alvin*.

http://www.panda.org/endangeredseas/
A news website that focuses on environmental issues relating
to the oceans – courtesy of the World Wide Fund for Nature.

http://www.mcsuk.org/
Information on how you can help conserve the oceans. Includes
details of beach cleanups and projects such as "Adopt a Turtle."

http://www.sharktrust.org/index.html
Fascinating facts about sharks and the problems they face due to
overfishing.

Please note: Every effort has been made to ensure that these websites
are suitable, and that their addresses are up-to-date at the time of going
to print. Website content is constantly updated, as are website addresses
– therefore, it is highly recommended that a responsible adult should visit
and check each website before allowing access to a child.

INDEX

A

Alaska, US 32, 38, 58, 62
algae 19, 37
ammonites 50
anchovies 9, 59
anemonefish 42-43
angelfish 20
anglerfish 6, 26
Antarctica 36-37, 54, 58
Apostles, Australia 10
aquaculture 52
Arabian Gulf 4
archaeology 50-51
Arctic Ocean 55, 58
Arctic tern 39
Atlantic Ocean 32, 38, 39
atolls, coral 18, 57
Australia 4, 10, 18, 22

B

bacteria 26, 31
Bahamas 11
Bardsey Island, Wales (UK) 14
barnacles 15, 43
barracuda 17
bathyscape 31, 62, 63
beaches 12-13
Beaufort scale 62
bioluminescence 26
birds 16, 24, 32, 34, 35, 38, 39, 55
black smokers 31
blenny 45
blowholes 11
blue holes 11
Boutan, Louis 48
breakers 8
breakwaters 10
Brent Spar 60

C

California 22-23, 41, 59
cameras, underwater 48
camouflage 25, 26, 45
carbon dioxide 20, 40, 58, 59
caves 11
Chesil Beach, Dorset (UK) 11
clams, giant 31, 52
cleaner fish 42, 45
cliffs 10, 14, 24
climate 4, 5, 56, 58
coasts 10-11, 32, 57
coconuts 32
Cocos Island, Costa Rica 21
cod 40, 54
color 7, 21, 26
cone shells 47
conservation 54-55
continents 4, 32
continental drift 4, 5
continental shelf 30
copepods 13, 40
coral reefs 4, 18-21, 42
    destruction of 19, 54, 55
corals, soft 21, 23
Cousteau, Jacques 59
crabs 14, 20, 29, 32, 36
    coconut 35

ghost 13
hermit 43
crocodiles 16
currents 5, 8, 9, 34, 39

D

deepsea zone 6, 28-29, 62
defenses, animal 45, 46
diatoms 40
dinoflagellates 47
divers 48-49
dodo 34
dolphins 6, 22, 40, 59

E

earthquakes 9, 32
East Pacific Rise 5
echinoderms 6
echo sounders 30, 63
eels 39, 44-45, 60
El Niño 59
energy, clean 59
erosion 10, 17
exploration 63

F

Fiennes, Sir Ranulph 38
Fiji 21, 31
finches 34
fish 6, 9, 22, 38, 40
    of Antarctic 36
    of coral reefs 20
    deepsea 28, 29
    mid-water 26
    shoals 6, 9, 24, 25, 56
    of shores 14, 15, 17
    survival methods 44-45
    venomous 47
fish farming 52, 53
Fisher, Mel 50
fishing 19, 30, 52, 54, 56
flashlight fish 26
flooding 17, 32
Florida, US 49, 50, 56
food chain 40
fossils 4, 50, 62
Fundy, Bay of, Canada 8, 62

G

Galápagos Islands 33, 34
gannets 35
geese 22
Genders, Sidney 38
glaciers 58
global warming 4, 20, 58-59
Gozo, Malta 11
gravity 8
Great Barrier Reef 4, 18
guillemots 24
Gulf Stream 5, 56
guyots 30, 31

H, I

Hawaii 8, 11, 12, 30, 55
herons 14
ice caps 58
icefish 36
Iceland 32
Indian Ocean 20, 46, 55
Indonesia 19, 32, 34, 55

insects 6, 32, 34
islands 18, 31-35, 57

J, K

jackfish 25, 43
Japan 9, 33, 54, 60
Japweed 60
jellyfish 6, 24, 25, 26, 43, 46, 62
kelp 14, 22-23, 41, 62
Komodo dragon 34
Komodo Island 19
Krakatoa 32
krill 37, 54

L

lava 30, 32, 33
light 7, 19, 24, 26, 40
limpets 15, 23, 25
lionfish 7, 47
lobsters 31, 39
lumpsucker 15
Lyme Regis, Dorset (UK) 50

M

magnetism, Earth's 38, 39
Malaysia 19, 32
Maldives 55
Malosteus 26
mangrove forests 16-17
Mariana Trench 31, 62
marine reserves 61
marram grass 13
Mary Rose 50
Mauritius 34
medicines 52
Mediterranean 8, 11
Mexico 38, 61
mid-ocean ridges 5, 30, 32
mid-water zone 6, 26-27
migration 16, 38-39, 62
monkeys 16
Moon 8
mountains 30, 32, 62
mud flats 10, 16
mudskippers 17
mussels 15, 52
mythology 62

N, O

natterjack toad 13
noise 59
Norway 9, 18, 54, 62
ocean floor 30
oceanography 56-57, 63
octopus 46, 47
oil spills 55, 57
Otto, Nikolaus 58
overfishing 52, 54, 56
oysters 53

P

Pacific Ocean 5, 18, 21, 46, 57, 59, 62, 63
pack ice 36, 37
Pangaea 4
Panthalassa 4
parasites 42
parrotfish 44
partnerships, animal 42-43
pearl farming 53

penguins 37
periwinkles 15, 52
Peru 9, 59
Philippines 19, 31, 34
photography 48, 57
photosynthesis 40
Phronima 26
Piccard, Jacques 31
piddocks 10
plankton 6, 7, 9, 21, 23, 24, 40-41, 47
plants 6, 13, 17, 32, 34, 40, 57, 60
plastic litter 61
pollution 54, 60-61
porcupinefish 45
pressure suits 49
pufferfish 45
puffins 60

R

rattail fish 6, 29
rays 41, 45
Red Sea 5, 20
reefs 4, 18-21, 42
remora 43
Remotely Operated Vehicles (ROVs) 31, 49
river deltas 10, 17
river estuaries 16
rock pools 14, 15
rocks 10, 14-15

S

salmon 38, 53
salt marshes 17
sand bars 10, 12
sand dunes 12-13
sandy shores 12-13
Sargasso Sea 25, 39
satellites 56, 57
scavengers 29
Scotland 18, 21, 35, 60
scuba diving 48, 63
sea anemones 15, 23, 29, 36, 42, 43
sea cows (dugongs) 22
sea cucumbers 6, 28, 29
sea dragons 45
sea grasses 22, 40
sea gypsies 52
seahorses 22
sea lavender 17
seals 12, 22, 36, 37, 55
sea mounts 31
sea otters 23, 41
sea pens 28, 29
sea scorpions 14
seashore 6, 12-17
sea slugs 43
sea snails 6, 14, 25
sea snakes 25, 46
sea spiders, giant 36
sea squirts 23, 26
sea urchins 6, 13, 20, 23, 25, 37, 41
sea walls 10
seaweed 14, 25, 40, 52
    see also kelp
Seychelles 35
sharks 17, 24, 29, 46, 56-57, 60
    basking 40
    blue 6, 39
    bluntnose six-gill 29

great white 40, 62
    hammerhead 45
    lemon 22
    megamouth 27
    reef 21
    whale 24
shellfish 10, 13, 14, 15, 47, 52
shingle bars 10, 11
shipwrecks 50
shrimp 26
silt 7
sonar 30, 56
sounds, whales 6, 62
Southeast Asia 19, 22, 52
sponges 20, 23, 52
squid 6, 26, 36, 62
starfish 6, 13, 15, 18, 20, 37
stonefish 47
submersibles 28, 29, 31, 49
sunlit zone 6, 24-25
surgeonfish 45
surfing 8-9
Surtsey Island, Iceland 32
surveys 57

T

tags, satellite 57
tectonic plates 5
temperatures, sea 56
tidal bores 62
tidal power 59
tides 8, 62
tourism 12, 34, 38, 49, 55, 60
treasure 50
trenches 5, 6, 30, 31, 62
tripodfish 28
tsunamis 9, 62
tube worms 21, 40
tuna 6, 56
turtles 25, 34, 39, 43, 60-61

V

venom 46-47, 62
vents 6, 31, 40, 63
visibility 7
volcanoes 18, 30, 31, 32-33

W

Wales 14, 55
Walsh, Donald 31
water pressure 7, 28
waves 8, 10, 11, 62
weather 5, 8
whales 6, 36, 38, 43, 59
    blue 6, 62
    gray 38, 62
    humpback 54-55
    killer 38
    sperm 7, 54, 62
whaling 54
whirlpools 9, 62
winds 8, 24, 59
World War II 50
worms 13, 21, 28, 40

ACKNOWLEDGMENTS

Dorling Kindersley would like to thank the following people for their help with this book: Andrew O'Brien for original digital artworks; Chris Bernstein for compiling the index; Caroline Bingham and Lisa Magloff for editorial assistance and proofreading; Janet Allis and Abbie Collinson for design assistance; Gemma Woodward for DK Picture Library research; the Sea Shepherd Organization, California, for supplying visual reference on Turtle Exclusion Devices (TEDs).

Dorling Kindersley would also like to thank the following for their kind permission to reproduce their photographs:

Key:
c = center; l = left; r = right;
b = bottom; t = top

Inside book credits:

Agence France Presse: 33br. **Ardea London Ltd:** Francois Gohier 6-7, 6-7, 38c, Adrian Warren 34clb. **British Museum:** 50bc. **Bruce Coleman Ltd:** Pacific Stock 55bc. **Coral Planet Photography:** Zafer Kizilkaya 55ca. **Corbis:** Tony Arruza 10clb; Lloyd Cluff 32bc; Amos Nachoum 1, 24bc; NASA / Corbis 17cr; Robert Pickett 11tr; Rick Price 36cl, 36clb; Paul A. Souders 34-35; Ralph White 29cr; Lawson Wood 11crb. **Dr. Frances Dipper:** 7clb, 21tr, 21cra, 50tr; 15tc; 34cra (turtle eggs). **David Doubilet:** 40-41. **Ecoscene:** Christine Osborne 53bl. **FLPA – Images of nature:** S. Jonasson 8cr; M. Jones / Minden Pictures 45cr; Minden Pictures 8-9; Silvestris Fotoservice 9tc; Skylight/FLPA 8clb, 8cb; Winifried Wisniewski 52cla. **Chris Gomersall**

Photography: 60bl, 11tl, 17tr. **The Image Bank / Getty Images:** Steven Hunt 45tr. **Jamstec:** 31tr. *Jules' Undersea Lodge:* 49br. **The Mary Rose Trust:** 50cla, 50c. **Dr. Mike Musyl:** 56br, 57bl, 57bc. **National Maritime Museum:** 50cl. **Natural History Museum:** 37crb. **Nature Picture Library:** Doug Allan 37cr; Nigel Bean 35tc; Bristol City Museum 34cla; Dan Burton 14clb, 40tr; Sue Daly 15br; Georgette Douwma 18cb, 44-45, 45cb, 48-49; Florian Graner 18bl; Jurgen Freud 9tr,15cr, 16br, 16-17, 32clb, 34ca; Tim Martin 39cla, 39cra; Pete Oxford 32-33, 35tr; Constantinos Petrinos 44tr; Michael Pitts 50cra; Jeff Rotman 20tr; Peter Scoones 45cra; Anup Shah 16bl; David Shale 25tr, 26c, 26c; Sinclair Stammers 26br; 39cra; Tom Vezo 34ca. **N.H.P.A.:** Agence Nature 21bc; Laurie Campbell 53cb; Trevor Macdonald 7bl; B. Jones & M. Shimlock 18-19, 51, 52-53; Alan Williams 16ca; Norbert Wu 28cl, 36-37, 36-37tc, 37cra, 61clb.

Oceanworks International Corporation: 49tc. **Oxford Scientific Films:** 60ca; Doug Allan 24cl; Ken Smith Laboratory / Scripps Inst. of Oceanography 31bc. **Pacific Tsunami Museum:** Cecilio Licos 9cr. **Phil Rosenberg:** 50tr. **Science Photo Library:** B. & C. Alexander 55tc; Martin Bond 59br; Bernhard Edmater 58-59; European Space Agency 56vla; Graham Ewens 10cla; Richard Folwell 49c; Simon Fraser 55br; Andrew J. Martinez 20bl; Douglas Faulkner 18c, 56-57; Dr. Ken Macdonald 5tr; Fred McConnaughey 39ca; B. Murion / Southampton Oceanography Centre 31br; Matthew Oldfield 7crb, 24-25; NASA 59ca; NOAA 56c; Nancy Sefton 2021; Andrew Syred 40bl. **Sue Scott:** 14cla. **Seapics.com:** Mark Colin 30-31; Saul Gonor 29tr; Richard Herrmann 62-63; Mako Hirose 56bl; Steven Kazlowski 54bc Rudie Kuiter 26cl; Doug Perrine 19cr, 25bl, 38-39, 49cra, 60-61; G. Brad Lewis 2-3; Bruce Rasner 27; James D. Watt 30bl. **Still Pictures:**

Kelvin Aitken 21bl; Fred Bavendam 4-5; Thomas Raupach 60bc; Norbert Wu 52cb. **Telegraph Color Library Getty Images:** Duncan Murrell 54-; **Visuals Unlimited:** David Wrobel 28bl, 28-29, 29br. **Woodfall Wild Images:** Nigel Bean 35tl; Inigo Eve 37br; Ted Mead 10-11; David Wood 10bl, 14-15.

Jacket credits:

Seapics.com: James D. Watt back flap/spine; Mark Cinlin back crb; Scripps Institution of Oceanography Gregory Ochocki back cbl. **FLPA – Images of nature:** Silvestris back c. **N.H.P.A.:** B. Jones & M. Shimlock b cb. **Stone / Getty Images:** Stuart Westmorland front.

All other images:

© Dorling Kindersley. For further information, see www.dkimages.com